Computers and the Primary Curriculum 3–13

for Jenny

Computers and the Primary Curriculum 3–13

edited by

Rob Crompton

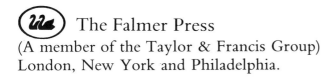 The Falmer Press
(A member of the Taylor & Francis Group)
London, New York and Philadelphia.

UK   The Falmer Press, Falmer House, Barcombe, Lewes, East Sussex, BN8 5DL

USA   The Falmer Press, Taylor & Francis Inc., 242 Cherry Street, Philadelphia, PA 19106-1906

First published 1989

British Library Cataloguing in Publication Data
Computers and the primary school curriculum 3–13
   Primary education. Applications of computer systems
   I. Crompton, Rob
   372'.028'5
   ISBN 1-85000-454-4

Library of Congress Cataloging in Publication Data is available on request

Jacket design by Caroline Archer

Typeset in 11/13 Bembo by Mathematical Composition Setters Ltd, Salisbury

Contents

Acknowledgements

The editor and contributors would like to thank all the children and teachers whose work is featured in this book, in particular those from the following schools:

All Saints Primary	Winchester
Alwyn Infants	Maidenhead
Crown Wood Primary	Bracknell
Emmbrook Infant	Wokingham
Fir Tree Lane Primary	Newbury
Foxborough Combined	Slough
Francis Baily Primary	Thatcham
Furze Platt Junior	Maidenhead
Geoffrey Field Junior	Reading
Guillemont Junior	Farnborough
Manor Infant	Reading
New Scotland Hill	Sandhurst
Oakley Junior	Basingstoke
Priory Combined	Burnham
Radstock Primary	Reading
Shaw House Comprehensive	Newbury
South Farnborough Junior	Farnborough
South Lake Junior	Reading
Victoria Park Nursery	Newbury
Whitelocke Infant	Wokingham

The editor is most grateful for the help and advice he has received from many colleagues, especially Roy Atherton, Carol Jewell, Margaret Johnson, Colin Monson, Jennie Moulton, and Chris Robson, and the visual aspects of this book were greatly enhanced by Peter Dixon, David Hinder and Brian Peters, whose creative flair and technical expertise are greatly appreciated. Tim Royle wishes to acknowledge the help of Ged Gast in preparing Chapter 12, and Anthony Hunt thanks Pauline Bleach, Andy Burford, Gerry Burnell, Pat Goodwin, Alan Melbourne, Pat Pysden and Lynne Smith for their assistance with Chapter 7.

1 Introduction: The Educational Context

Rob Crompton

Although this introduction is positioned as one would expect, at the beginning of the book, it is quite likely that many readers will come to it after dipping into the pages which follow. If that is the case then the prime purpose of the book will have been achieved, that is, to produce a readily accessible source of ideas, and essentially practical suggestions for busy primary school teachers. Nevertheless, it is hoped that this section will be found helpful, as some of the issues about the use of computers in schools are discussed, and some general principles are identified.

It could be argued of course that only a foolish person would attempt to write a book in such a rapidly developing field. No sooner had the ink dried, the text would be out of date! Although there is no reason to suppose that, to some extent at least, this will not be true of this present volume, the contributors share some confidence that a 'best before' date stamped on the back would not be appropriate, and there are various reasons for this view:

(i) There is currently wide agreement about the appropriate use of computers in primary schools, and the basic philosophy is unlikely to change despite the anticipated (and unforeseen) technological developments over the next few years.

(ii) The existing BBC machines which the overwhelming majority of schools have acquired during the last few years are unlikely, given financial constraints, to be replaced in the immediate future by more powerful models. They are going to be around, and remain extremely effective, for some years hence. Most likely, there will be a parallel development, not a replacement.

> There is no successor to the general purpose BBC Master ... the strength of third party support, especially for primary, and the add-ons from Concept Keyboards to music processors means the BBC machines will run and run. (Quinn, 1988)

(iii) Although some schools are beginning to acquire more powerful computers, the publication of specially written software, particularly for primary schools, is likely to take some time. However, in the interim period many existing programs written in BBC Basic can now be used with the Nimbus and Archimedes machines. This is an argument for parallelism and continuity.

(iv) The practical suggestions relating to curriculum content, organization and teaching strategies can be easily modified to accommodate the emerging, more sophisticated, resources.

Philosophy

It is not possible, of course, to discuss 'the philosophy of computers in the primary school' without first identifying some underlying assumptions about primary education in general. Thus the main functions of this introduction are to discuss some aspects of 'good practice' and to highlight some basic principles in the use of computers in primary schools.

Teaching Style

The debate about traditional/progressive methods must surely be regarded as redundant. Recent evidence has shown that many teachers adapt their style according to the nature of the curriculum area in hand, and the ORACLE (Galton and Simon, 1980) studies have demonstrated the folly of associating a particular style of teaching with particular learning outcomes. Thus the 'progressive' teacher may largely be involved in managing a complex array of activities, whereas the 'traditional' teacher may be using a far wider range of higher-order questioning techniques.

The Reflective Practitioner

A most useful phrase which is becoming widely used in the context of teaching style is 'the reflective practitioner'. One would expect, of course, that teachers would 'think about what they are doing', and indeed the likelihood of meeting a teacher who maintained the same curriculum diet, without responding in some way to the needs of the particular group of children, must be very remote.

However, rather than being simply patronizing, the concept is very useful and has been the basis of some most interesting and practical suggestions by, among others, Joan Dean (1983) and Andrew Pollard and Sarah Tann (1987).

In her book *Organising Learning in the Primary School Classroom*, Joan Dean provides a series of checklists or matrices which the teacher can use to review his or her own practice and suggests a number of criteria for the evaluation of classroom strategies. For example she suggests the following headings for the analysis of teaching methods and succinctly sums up her view thus: 'There is no one right method of teaching. It is probably better to use a variety'.

12	11	10	9	8	7	6	5	4	3	2	1		
												Talking/listening to class/group	
												Organising activity	
												Radio, TV, films	Class or group activities
												Leading practical work	
												Questioning/ discussion	
												Other activities	
												Explaining to individuals	
												Talking/listening to individuals	Contacts with individuals
												Checking work hearing reading	
												Other activities	

Analysis 8 Teacher's Time Log   Name:.........   Date:.........

The management of learning

By kind permission of Croom Helm

Andrew Pollard and Sarah Tann in their more recent book, *Reflective Teaching in the Primary School*, also provide a number of useful practical activities through which teachers can analyze their own practice. One of the activities for example involves the examination of classroom tasks in terms of their learning demands, and is shown below.

PRACTICAL ACTIVITY 6.8

Aim: To examine tasks in terms of their learning demands.

Method: Analyse the demands of each task set during the day by using the grid below:

Task Type

	Incremental (new skills acquired in task)	Restructuring (known skills advanced in task)	Enrichment (known skills applied in task)	Practice (known skills assumed in task)	Revision (known skills reactivated in task)
Task no. 1 2 3 4 5					

Having analysed the tasks, then ask the children for their views (using terms which they would recognize) about which kind of tasks they thought they were doing.

Follow-up: From this evidence, what can you deduce about the match or mismatch in the classroom? Can you identify the reasons for it? What can you do about it?

By kind permission of Cassell Education

A further source of guidance for teachers can be found in *Teaching Infants* by Trevor Kelly and Janice Tollitt (1987) who again provide a series of tasks for the teacher to complete. An example of their approach is their 'Grouping for learning' task below.

 Task 4 Grouping for learning

1   Take a look at the structure of your own school: the number of pupils on roll, the number of classes into which they are divided, the age and/or ability criteria which inform this division into classes. It might help to draw a diagram of the school organisation showing this information.
2   Now consider your own classroom. Note the age-range of pupils in your class. What mechanisms do you use to assign the children to working groups eg age, sex, ability, interest? Do you use a variety of methods?
3   Take each of the grouping methods you have listed in response to 2 above, and say why you use it and under what circumstances.

By kind permission of Basil Blackwell

As can be seen from the above examples, implicit in the concept of the 'reflective practitioner' are certain underlying assumptions about what the practitioner should think *about*.

The Official View

The Educational Reform Act 1988 prescribes the subjects to be included in the curriculum of all state primary schools. At the time of writing three reports are available which, although comments are invited, are likely to form the basis of the National Curriculum: the reports by the Working Groups on Mathematics and Science, and the report by the Committee of Inquiry into the Teaching of English (The Kingman Report). All three reports contain many recommendations concerning knowledge and content — attainment targets, profile components, programmes of study etc, and all three contain explicit references to teaching methods.

Guidelines for Programmes of Study

8.10 The work which a teacher designs for a class of pupils will consist of a set of varied activities designed to help pupils to achieve the next levels in attainment targets. The activities will involve pupils in 'chalk and talk' with teachers, as well as in individual and group work, involving pencil and paper, practical work and private study. These activities will be sparked by the full range of stimuli deployed in the good classroom, not least by pupil initiative. They will involve work in and beyond the classroom designed to improve knowledge and skills.

Mathematics for Ages 5 to 16 (Proposals for the National Curriculum)

There are also a number of references to the use of computers, for example: 'Children's (*7 to 11 years*) work in a wide variety of areas should incorporate the use of information technology for storing, processing, retrieving and presenting information, and for simple control applications' (Science Report); and: 'Create shapes (*Level 4, Algebra*) by use of DRAW and MOVE commands in the appropriate graphics mode, or using logo' (Mathematics Report).

Such examples seem to indicate that the National Curriculum will reflect and incorporate many of the ideas and methods that have been identified as 'good practice' by previous government publications, although the Secretary of State has expressed some reservations regarding the process aspects of the reports. Also, of course, it has been argued that the imposition of regular testing may greatly influence the methodology adopted by schools. However, the report of the Task Group on Assessment and Testing, issued in 1988, attempted to resolve the 'widely voiced fear that external tests will impose arbitrary restrictions

Exploration and Investigation: Doing

ATTAINMENT TARGET 17

Pupils should develop skills of planning and carrying out explorations, investigations and tasks and interpreting and evaluating outcomes.

RELEVANT PART OF THE PROGRAMME OF STUDY

5 to 7

On the basis of work carried out in the programme of study children should be involved in direct interaction with materials and objects in their environment, gaining information by wide–ranging observations using all senses in ways which are safe and appropriate [1], [10], [14].

They should be encouraged to raise questions, and where appropriate become involved in finding answers to them by investigation.

7 to 11

On the basis of work carried out in the programmes of study children should be encouraged to become more systematic in their exploration and investigation. There should be opportunities for:

– exploring phenomena and undertaking surveys [1], [4];

– testing ideas, models and predictions [5], [10];

– making comparisons [1], [2] and evaluating materials, structures and devices [11].

In these explorations and investigations children should be involved in making observations which are progressively more detailed and more quantitative [9].

They should be encouraged to reflect critically on their results and on the way in which these have been obtained and to use this experience in improving later procedures.

Science for Ages 5 to 16
(Proposals for the National Curriculum)

Teaching and learning

2.5   The National Association of Advisers in English has published a statement, written by David Allen, which sums up the characteristics of successful language teaching:

"The main job of the teacher responsible for the growth and development of pupils' language is to enable the child to speak, listen, read and write effectively. To do this successfully, teachers need to organise the learning in ways which follow on logically and consistently from the successful language learning which children have already accomplished in the context of their own homes and communities: learning to speak their parents' language, whether that be English or any other first language. This means that school learning must retain the essential features of this learning, which are:

1. A very high expectation of success for the learner.
2. An "apprenticeship" approach to acquiring written and oral language, in which the adult represents the "success" the child seeks and yet offers endless help.
3. Maximum encouragement and support whilst errors are mastered.
4. Motivation for the learner to make sense of and acquire control over language and the power which it can have.
5. A constant respect for the child's language."

English for Ages 5 to 16 (Proposals for the National Curriculum)

on teachers' own work, and so limit and devalue their professional role'.

Since the publication of *The Primary Survey* in 1978 there has been a plethora of documents emanating from the DES. *The Practical Curriculum* was closely followed by *Primary Practice* and then the series of discussion documents entitled *Curriculum Matters* which were intended to contribute to the process of establishing general agreement about curricular aims and objectives. The 1988 Act of course somewhat accelerated the progress towards common aims!

Consistent across all recent government publications, including to a large extent the reports on mathematics, science and English mentioned above, is the notion that the curriculum should have certain characteristics: Breadth, Balance, Relevance,

Differentiation, Progression and Continuity. There also seems to be much agreement about the usefulness, when considering aims and objectives, of thinking in terms of Knowledge, Skills, Attitudes and Concepts.

How Can the Computer Help to Ensure Such Characteristics and Support Such a Variety of Aims?

The chapters which follow this introduction contain many practical suggestions which may help teachers to achieve many of these laudable outcomes but it is perhaps useful to briefly summarize the possible role of the computer under these headings.

Breadth

Although it has been argued that some teachers will find the demands of the National Curriculum restrictive, and some may be tempted to confine their teaching to the elements they know will be tested, the legislation may at least ensure that all children will come into contact with a range of learning and experience. And there is nothing in the Act which precludes teachers from adopting an integrated approach. The time required for the various subjects is described in percentage terms rather than hours per week, and so the practice adopted by many schools of giving emphasis to different things from term to term may well continue.

The computer can play a major role in supporting a thematic approach, both as a resource for storing and sorting information and in providing the central starting point or focus of a topic and these aspects are fully explored later in this book (Chapters 5, 6, 7 and 8). When attempting to provide a broad range of experiences for children it is sometimes difficult to avoid a somewhat superficial coverage, and to ensure that they have opportunities to study at a depth appropriate to their stage of development. It is here that the judicial use of the computer can be very effective, which brings us to an important point of principle:

THE PLACE OF THE COMPUTER IS IN THE CLASSROOM

If children have access to a computer for a short period of time then there is a danger of it being used for nothing more than 'drill and practice'. Although this is a legitimate function of the computer, which can provide opportunities to make such exercises match individual needs, the use of the machine exclusively for such activities would be regrettable. There is a temptation for teachers to distribute the allocated day equally among all the children in the class, often by loading a program on the morning and organizing a series of very short sessions during the course of the day. It *is* possible to use the computer purposefully even when time is limited and Anthony Hunt suggests some strategies in Chapter 7. The central point is that the computer should be part of the general learning environment either in the classroom or in an adjacent space.

If the computer is housed in a 'computer room', library or resource area it is often difficult to arrange a reasonable level of supervision and frequently means that children are directed to the computer for short periods. The 'ten minute turn' syndrome is then difficult to avoid.

It is quite natural for a school to try and distribute computer time fairly and provide equal opportunities for all the children. With only one or two machines and a large number of children the problem is real. Even so, a more appropriate strategy is to assign a computer to a class, or to a team, for extended periods of anything from a week to half a term. This arrangement means that teachers can plan their use of the computer in some detail, and there seems to be a general consensus among experienced micro users that a sustained period of time is more effective than the equivalent period divided into one or two day periods. Of course the consequence of this is that there will be sustained periods when children have no access at all, but until schools are funded more generously this must be accepted as a modest price for more effective use of limited resources.

Balance

It is tempting, especially in the light of recent legislation, to think that the control of balance has been removed from the class teacher. However, the concept is more useful than simply the determination of proportions of time given to the *content* of the curriculum, and even in this narrow definition there is no suggestion that children should experience the required 'diet' of subjects every week.

Perhaps more important than curriculum balance from the point of view of the child, is the balance of experience and activity. Consider this 'well balanced' day ...

9.00–9.30	Assembly
9.30–10.30	Language (Ginn 360)
10.30–10.50	Break (indoors due to rain)
10.50–12.00	Mathematics (Peak)
12.00–1.30	Lunch (20 minutes outdoors)
1.30–2.00	Music (in hall)
2.00–3.00	Topic ('Space')
3.00–3.20	Story (BFG)

... and its implications for the child's experience:

School Day	Child's Experience
9.00–9.30	Assembly sitting/listening/singing
9.30–10.30	Language (Ginn 360) sitting/reading/writing
10.30–10.50	Break (indoors) sitting/reading/drawing
10.50–12.00	Mathematics (Peak) sitting/reading/writing
12.00–1.30	Lunch (20 mins. outdoors) sitting/eating/playing
1.30–2.00	Music (in hall) sitting/reading/singing
2.00–2.30	Topic ('Space') sitting/reading/painting
3.00–3.30	Story (BFG) sitting/listening

Although this might be considered a little contrived, it does serve to highlight the need to think of balance in a wider sense.

'Balance need not be sought over a single week or even a single month since in some cases it may be profitable to concentrate in depth on certain activities' (Curriculum 5–13, p.113)

The following headings may be useful:

ACTIVITY

Reading	Writing
literature/information	personal/factual
Talking	**Listening**
to teachers/to peers	to teacher/to peers/to radio
formal/informal	for pleasure/for information

DISCUSSING

direct experience   practical activity   vicarious experience
making   creating   investigating   reasoning   deciding
problem-solving   cooperating   individual work
time 'alone'   computing   watching TV   concentrating
relaxing sitting moving being quiet/loud being challenged
role playing   playing   being directed   choosing   deciding

The computer can provide an extra dimension to the child's work and can facilitate almost all the learning experiences in the above list.

Relevance

It would be easy to take for granted the relevance of working with computers in the classroom: 'this is the age of the silicon chip' and 'soon everything will be computerized' are phrases often heard. There is probably much truth here of course but in addition to being relevant to future activities and to the 'technological revolution', the computer provides opportunities for ensuring relevance which is not deferred to some point in the future when the children begin to experience 'life'. As has been said so aptly 'childhood is not a rehearsal for life — children are living now!'

One example of this is the use of a simple word-processing program by a child who has great difficulty in writing neatly. Another is the use of a database to record weather conditions, compare with previous years, and to predict the likelihood of a dry fete, sports day or cricket match. Again, children faced with a real problem involving Design Technology, for example the need for a switching device, would certainly be involved in 'relevant' activities. The ways in which such experiences can be inherently motivating are fully described by Pat Williams and David Jinks in *Design Technology 5–12* (1985).

Differentiation

There are a number of strategies which can be adopted to achieve differentiation in the classroom. In order to provide for a wide range of developmental stages, interests, and learning styles one can, for example:

(i)   set individual tasks for each child

(ii) set up homogeneous groups and provide appropriate tasks for each group

(iii) set up mixed groups and provide common tasks and experiences to which each child can respond at his or her own level.

It is quite likely that teachers will adopt each of these strategies from time to time, and of course this list is not exhaustive. Although one can rationalize teaching styles for the purpose of analysis, in practice there must be a huge range of techniques in use in primary schools, as teachers attempt to provide an appropriately differentiated curriculum for their pupils.

The computer can be a very useful resource in the context of differentiation because many programs can be adjusted in terms of ability level, speed, number of stages or loops involved, and, as is often observed, the micro does not become frustrated or lose patience. Furthermore, children often seem to enjoy computer tasks which might induce boredom if presented in some other way. Unfortunately boredom is exactly what was achieved by some writers of the early programs. Some of their efforts were not inspiring and had the effect of deterring many teachers just as computers were appearing in schools. Happily this phase was shortlived and although some inferior programs are still used, there is now a wide range of well produced and easily obtainable software available to teachers. A glance at the chapters which follow this introduction will reveal the variety of ways in which the computer can assist in providing a differentiated curriculum, and there are many examples of how children have responded according to their ability, experience and interest to programs involving problem-solving, data collection, word processing etc.

It is appropriate here to mention another point of principle. Quite understandably, a teacher who is trying to tailor a task to the needs of an individual child may think it logical for the child to work individually at the computer.

The computer is very powerful in generating genuine involvement

Whilst there may be occasions when this is appropriate, and there will certainly be times when children ask to work by themselves, a general rule is to

AVOID HAVING ONE CHILD WORKING ALONE

A feature of most primary classrooms today is the modular arrangement of the furniture, and among the reasons for this is the desire among teachers to facilitate language development

and to encourage children to work in a cooperative way with their peers; addressing problems, exchanging ideas, making hypotheses, drawing conclusions, and so on. The ORACLE studies (Galton and Simon, 1980) served to confirm what many teachers had found: that it was more difficult to promote cooperative group work than the Plowden Report (CACE, 1967) had implied.

In contrast, a common feature of the case studies described in the following chapters is the amount of group work which the various activities involved. It seems that the computer is very powerful in generating genuine involvement and commitment, and can enhance those language and social skills which most teachers seek to develop in their children.

Having decided that children should normally work in groups for activities involving the computer, the next decision to make is on the composition of such groups. Although there are many permutations one thing seems to be clear:

DO NOT LEAVE THE GROUPING OF CHILDREN TO CHANCE

Some extremely interesting suggestions in relation to grouping can be found in *Equal Opportunities and Computer Education in the Primary School* (Judith Ellis, 1987) which summarizes the project set up by the Equal Opportunities Commission.

Grouping the Children to Use the Computer in the Classroom

WHAT TO DO

Decide how many children there are going to be in each of the groups. The number of children in each group may not be equal and will depend upon:

the children's age

the software the children are going to use

the number of tasks that have been identified for the children to do

the number of children in the class and the amount of computer time available

the number of children who can sit comfortably at the computer

Decide which children are to be in each of the groups; this will depend upon:

whether the child is a girl or a boy

their age

their reading age

their ability

their previous computer experience

their personality

Observing the Children Using the Computer in the Classroom

WHAT TO DO

Make time to observe each group working at the computer. Try to make the first observation soon after they have started so there is still time to intervene.

Look out for a child in the group taking over by:

    making decisions alone

    monopolising the keyboard

    operating the keyboard too quickly

    telling the other children what to do

Look out for the child in the group being left out by:

    the other children ignoring them

    losing interest

    disagreeing with the other children

    not understanding what the other children are doing

Be aware of unrest within a group.

Be prepared to intervene and stop unacceptable behaviour where the children in the group are not each getting their equal turn at the computer

Be flexible, alter the groupings.

⊜ Observe the girls in both the single-sex and mixed groups.

⊜ Look out for:

    girls who are not operating the keyboard for their fair share of the time

    girls who are letting other children tell them what to do

    girls whose ideas are nearly always rejected by the rest of the group irrespective of whether they are right or wrong

    girls who choose to read the screen or record the information even when the group has been told to share the tasks

And ask yourself why?

Although the project set out to investigate issues relating to gender and the use of computers in the primary classrooms, Judith Ellis observes that

> it may be surprising that more of the guidelines do not refer specifically to the position of girls and women teachers but the issues that are important to equality of opportunity are the very same issues that are important to good primary practice

and indeed the summary document contains many useful ideas in relation to using a computer in the classroom. On the subject of grouping the EOC project found that three was probably the optimum number of junior-age children to be working together at a 'computer station': one child to read the screen, one to operate the keyboard, and one to make notes, the group rotating so that each child has the opportunity to perform all three tasks.

Whilst this is a very useful starting point when deciding on appropriate groups, there are of course a number of factors to consider; for example the project found that younger children worked better together in groups of two. Many of the recommendations are summarized in freely copyable form at the end of the document and those relating to grouping are reproduced above.

Progression and Continuity

Many schools are currently addressing the issues of progression and continuity. Circular 6/81, which required LEAs to publish curriculum guidelines, accelerated the move towards agreed curriculum policies which many schools had been working on for some time, and despite the difficulty in organizing staff discussions due to the concurrent dispute about pay and conditions of service, a remarkable degree of success appeared to have been achieved. For example, a number of schools drew up plans for project work which ensured that children would be introduced to a hierarchy of skills and a variety of experience during a period of years.

Fortunately, as far as work with computers is concerned, the need to provide a range of programs in a particular genre has been identified. Many of the chapters which follow emphasize this concern for progression, for example a hierarchy of word processing programs is identified by Philip Mann when discussing language work in Chapter 4.

One of the aims of the National Curriculum is to ensure that a child moving from one phase of education to another, or from one school to another, can do so without the trauma of finding that what has been learned in one school has not been appropriate as preparation for the next. Many schools had already recognized the problem and were devising schemes to ensure continuity within their own establishments well before the new Act. It must be said, however, that the emergence of computers in primary schools did not, at first, help in this. It was not uncommon to visit a school and to be shown a vast collection of colour-coded programs which were usually cassette-based. A visit to a neighbouring school would often reveal a similar collection — but with completely different programs!

Thankfully this is no longer a typical scenario, and more and more schools are concluding that rather than attempt to become familiar with a vast collection of software they should concentrate on building up experience and expertise in using a more limited range of programs and in gathering together supporting material. The teacher who is familiar with a data-handling program, a word-processing package and an adventure/simulation game has a powerful extension to the teaching strategies available. An example of this approach is discussed by Denby Richards in Chapter 13.

When the school policy is to ensure that all teachers share a working knowledge of a finite number of programs, it is much easier to achieve progression and continuity. For example, in the area of data collection and interpretation, young children could use OURFACTS, and progress to programs such as GRASS or INFORM. Also, the practice of a number of LEAs in subsidizing and providing INSET support for a particular set of programs is likely to ease the problem of transfer from school to school. This spiral approach to the development of information skills is discussed further by David Cowell in Chapter 8.

Knowledge, Skills, Concepts and Attitudes

The main body of this book contains numerous practical suggestions for teachers who are endeavouring to achieve aims which could be categorized using the four headings above. It is important, however, that this classification of aims does not impose an artificial sub-division of the curriculum. It is not really possible to teach knowledge one day and 'skills' the next! There is nothing one can suggest which children should be able to do without understanding — or that they should understand without having acquired the appropriate conceptual framework. Useful as it is for analysis, it is simply a theoretical device and should not necessarily imply a timetable consisting of periods devoted to promoting 'attitudes' in isolation from the other aspects of the curriculum.

Conclusion

Whilst the possibilities for enhancing and enriching the curriculum with the use of computers have been explored in this introduction, and are further developed throughout the book, the introduction of a computer in the classroom is not, of course, a universal panacea for all problems. And it is highly unlikely that it will mean less work for the teacher. This idea really belongs to the realms of mythology. The micro will not completely ease the burden on teachers in relation to satisfying the demands of the National Curriculum, in making sure that all the children are well behaved, attentive and realizing their potential, and in convincing parents that they are totally committed to such aims. It will probably help in all these things but what it will certainly do, if used with sensitivity, is to greatly enhance the educational process for both teachers and children.

Future Developments

If the publication of a book about computers is fraught with the difficulties described earlier, then the inclusion of a section on future developments deserves to be regarded as foolhardy! A whole book could of course be devoted to describing the current state-of-the-art computers, the possibilities opened up by the universal adoption of electronic mail and the provision of Interactive Video in every classroom. The difference the advent of WIMP (Windows, Icons, Mouse, Printer) technology is beginning to make in the classroom could also be discussed and the demise of the QWERTY keyboard could be suitably celebrated. However, the intention of this particular volume is to provide an overview of the use of computers across the primary curriculum and the anticipated readership consists of students in initial training, teachers who have absolutely no experience, and those who have made a start but who require some practical ideas in order to widen their expertise. What will the immediate future hold for them? Unless there is a huge input of funds similar to the Department of Industry scheme which had such a dramatic effect on the use of computers in schools, and unless resources can be found to support the handful of superb writers of educational software we have in this country, then the future is reasonably predictable. The new hardware will be available to larger institutions and only a few machines will end up in the primary sector where most of the software available will be simply conversions of existing programs. Ironically, it has been argued that the new generation computers should be available, at first, to primary schools where computing is very much cross-curricular, rather than to secondary schools where less sophisticated machines can be used for elementary computer studies, and the integration of computers across the whole curriculum is not so far advanced.

However, the future is not altogether depressing. The money that has been made available, under the Educational Support

Grant scheme, for the establishment of computer support teams, will enable far more classroom teachers to consolidate and enhance their expertise, and provide opportunities for the team members themselves to develop and extend their strategies for course planning and leadership. It is to be hoped that the pioneering work done by the MEP programme which achieved so much with relatively few resources will be an inspiration to these ESG teams and the MESU (Microelectronics in Education Support Unit).

Again, a number of LEAs have formed consortia in order to produce support materials and new programs, an example of this cooperation being the RESOURCE group, an association of northern counties based in Doncaster which has produced some extremely useful software and supplementary information.

The essential message to those new to the world of educational computing is that, despite the constraints mentioned above, there are plenty of people around who can offer help and advice. The benefits in terms of the enhancement of the curriculum for the children, and the professional satisfaction from doing so, are enormous.

> *From sand is the silicon microcircuit created, from sand the optical fibre. The most common and worthless material about us, available in inexhaustible quantities, suddenly is transformed to be the key to all our futures, in a world so different from the one we know that merely to turn our minds to it stuns our imaginations. The task of education in helping our kind to make the transition to a new lifestyle is one which will demand all our skills, insights, flexibility. Yet the role of education is central for it is in the mind of man that the revolution to come will be fought... In the kingdom of sand all things become possible, and only the imagination rules.* (Professor W. Gosling, 1978)

References

Central Advisory Council for Education (CACE) (1967) *Children and their Primary Schools* (The Plowden Report) London, HMSO.

Dean, J. (1983) *Organising Learning in the Primary School Classroom*, Beckenham, Croom Helm.

DES (1978) *Primary Education in England*, London, HMSO.

DES (1985) *The Curriculum 5 to 16*, London, HMSO

DES (1988a) *Mathematics for Ages 5 to 16 (Proposals for the National Curriculum)*, London, HMSO.

DES (1988b) *English for Ages 5 to 11 (Proposals for the National Curriculum)*, London, HMSO.

DES (1988c) *Science for Ages 5 to 16 (Proposals for the National Curriculum*, London, HMSO.

Ellis, Judith (1987) *Equal Opportunities and Computer Education in the Primary School*, Equal Opportunities Commission.

Galton, M. and Simon, B. (1980) *Progress and Performance in Primary Classrooms*, London, Routledge and Kegan Paul.

Gosling, W. (1978) *Microcomputers in Education: A Set of Introductory Articles*, Council for Educational Technology.

Kelly, T., and Tollitt, J. (1987) *Teaching Infants*, Basil Blackwell.

Pollard, A. and Tann, S. (1987) *Reflective Teaching in the Primary School*, London, Cassell.

Quinn, T. (1988) Hardware in Practice, in *Educational Computing*, September, Redwood.

Schools Council (1981) *The Practical Curriculum*, London, Methuen Education.

Schools Council (1983) *Primary Practice*, London, Methuen Education.

Williams, P. and Jinks, D. (1985) *Design & Technology 5–12*, Lewes, Falmer Press.

2 Getting Started

Howard Gillings and David Griffiths

The thought of using a computer in any way is something that can cause concern to a large number of people. This may be caused by unhelpful contact with the products of computers. We have all heard stories of the grossly incorrect bill and the difficulties people have encountered in getting mistakes put right, or maybe have seen images on film of powerful machines that go haywire or of programmers typing in vast amounts of unintelligible commands to make the machine work. These experiences give many people the impression that computers are complicated, unfriendly, unforgiving machines. It is not, however, the computer that is at fault — it is the program that it is using. The program is simply a list of instructions written in such a way that the computer 'understands' them and produces the result the programmer wants. Sometimes programmers make mistakes!

The alternative view of computers is that they are now a common and essential adjunct to modern life and are used by most people either directly or indirectly every day — the cash dispenser at the bank, the pay desk in the supermarket or department store, the video recorder and the automatic washing machine are a few of the instances where a computer is in common use. In most of these cases it is not obvious that it is a computer that is at the heart of the process. Most of these contacts with computers are useful and straightforward and hold no fears for most people, because the computer is programmed to be easy to use, and it is now increasingly the case that computers are being programmed with ease of use being a major consideration. This is the key pointer towards using computers in primary schools — the programs used should be simple to use, relevant and useful.

Using the computer in the classroom should be looked on in a similar way to using other equipment such as the cassette recorder, the video recorder or the slide projector. It should be simply a matter of switching on and then using suitable programs that have been provided. There is absolutely no need for teachers to learn how to program the computer — that is a job for expert programmers. After all we do not normally expect teachers to write the books, film the television programmes or take the photographs they use in school! Teachers should use their expertise as professional educationalists to make sound educational use of the computer and its associated programs within the curriculum.

Hardware and Software

The difference has already begun to emerge between the computer and the programs it uses. The common jargon used calls the different items of equipment the hardware — this includes such items as the computer, the monitor and the printer — while the programs the computer uses are called the software.

The Hardware — The Computer System

Although there are many different designs of computer systems on the market, a typical system consists of the computer and its keyboard, a TV or monitor and a disc drive or cassette recorder. There may be other items of hardware such as a printer or a concept keyboard attached to the computer. In order to keep things as clear as possible, and bearing in mind that it is by far

The hardware: on the bottom shelf, the computer/keyboard and the disc drive, on the top shelf, the monitor and printer

the most common computer in primary schools, we shall be using the BBC Model B computer as the 'standard' computer in schools and give our advice accordingly. However, if you have a different system, the relationship between the various parts is exactly the same.

The Computer and the Keyboard

The computer itself is a fawn coloured box with a typewriter-type keyboard on the top and a number of sockets on the back and underneath. Inside the box is a number of microchips and circuit boards which make the computer work. There is no need for you to attempt to understand how they work!

The BBC keyboard

Although the keyboard is similar to that of a typewriter there are a number of specialist keys that require a brief explanation.

The key that will probably be used most is the RETURN key on the right of the keyboard. This is the key used to confirm an action — normally the computer will wait for this key to be pressed before carrying out an instruction you have typed in.

The SHIFT and SHIFT LOCK keys act in the same way as those keys on a typewriter giving capital letters and the upper character on the key when the key has two characters assigned to it. When SHIFT LOCK is activated a red light glows at the bottom left of the keyboard.

The CAPS LOCK has a similar light which indicates when the key is activated. This allows you to type in capitals and type the lower character on keys where there is a choice. If both indicator lights are out then you can type in lower case and use the lower character on a key where there is a choice.

The brown keys with arrows on them on the right of the keyboard are called the CURSOR keys and are frequently used in programs to move around the screen.

The row of red keys across the top of the keyboard are called the FUNCTION keys and are used for a variety of purposes in many of the programs you will use. Normally such programs will provide a strip of card to line up with the keys to indicate their use.

The CTRL or control key on the left of the keyboard is only ever used in conjunction with other keys and should not be used unless the program requires it.

The ESCAPE key to the top left of the keyboard is often used to help you use a program effectively but as it can also cause you to finish a program you should use it only when the program instructions tell you to.

The BREAK key will normally take you out of a program or at the least back to the beginning and should not be pressed without thought for the likely dire consequences!

The Monitor

In order to see how the computer is responding it is essential to connect it up to a suitable colour monitor. Although a television can be used, the monitor is the normal way for you to see the result of your interaction with the computer.

The Disc Drive

In order to use programs it is essential to connect either a cassette recorder or a disc drive to the computer. When BBC computers originally arrived in schools, cassettes were used to store programs. Fortunately this slow unreliable medium has now been replaced in most schools by the floppy disc and its related disc drive. We shall deal in more detail with discs and disc drives later on in the chapter.

These three items make up the basic computer system. Many schools add other items of hardware to this system.

The Printer

One of the most common extra items of hardware is the printer. This is used to obtain a printout of work that the children have done, either text or pictures depending on the type of program being used, or for printing out information stored by the computer.

The Concept Keyboard

It has been found helpful, particularly with young children or with children with special needs, to allow communication with the computer that does not rely on the typewriter keyboard. The Concept Keyboard is a board which is covered with pressure sensitive squares which can be programmed to respond to a child's touch, thus removing dependence on the normal keyboard. The Concept Keyboard can be covered by a variety of overlays with words or pictures on them which when pressed send whole words or phrases to the computer. These overlays are either provided with the appropriate programs or can be made up by the class teacher to suit individual children. A detailed account of the potential of the Concept Keyboard can be found in Chapter 10.

Using the System

Before guiding you through the necessary steps to get the computer working it is necessary to look in more detail at the way programs can be accessed.

Using Discs

We have already seen that the computer needs a list of instructions called a program to make it work. If you had to type in all these instructions each time you wanted to use the computer there would be no demand for computers anywhere! Fortunately once a program is written it can be saved and then used again at a later date. Programs are saved electronically on magnetically sensitive material either on a cassette identical to an ordinary audio cassette or on a disc of the same material, normally called a floppy disc.

The discs used with the BBC Micro are 5.25″ in diameter and are enclosed in a slim cardboard case, usually black. The whole thing comes with a paper dust cover which should be used at all times when the disc is not in use. The disc within the cardboard cover is made of the same type of material as a cassette tape and is therefore able to store information in a similar way. Each disc has to be prepared by the computer before it can be used. This is called formatting. Once the disc is formatted it can be used to store programs and information for future use. Recently a new type of disc has become available. This is the 3.5″ disc which comes in a hard plastic case and is consequently more robust. It does, of course, require a different type of disc drive. There is more detailed information about discs and disc drives in Chapter 14 on 'Technical Tips'.

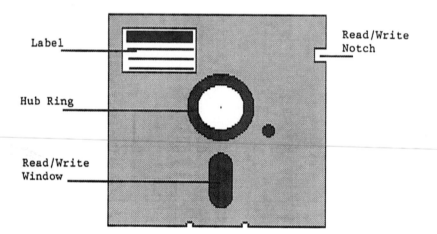

A 5.25″ disc

The disc drive and the Disc Filing System within the computer allow you to store information on the disc and retrieve information from it. To begin with most of your contact with discs will involve retrieving information stored on the disc by someone else. When you retrieve this information the computer is actually reading a copy of the program into its memory and leaving the original in place on the disc. In this way you can use the same program many times without any difficulty. A suitable analogy to this would be that of listening to a record or watching a video: you may do either many times without wiping out the original. The majority of commercially produced discs are set up to start automatically, either with the program you require or with a menu of programs for you to select from, if you press the appropriate keys.

Running a Program

Before attempting to use the system make sure all the hardware is switched on. You will probably be using a system that is already connected up correctly. If the system is not connected together you should refer either to the chapter on Technical Tips or to a colleague to obtain help.

Once you have switched on you will hear a two-tone beep and have some writing on the monitor screen which will look something like this:

BBC Computer 32K
Acorn DFS
BASIC
>

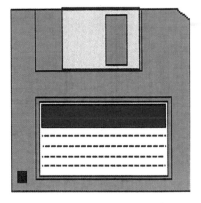

A 3.5" disc

The > is the prompt the computer gives you to indicate it is ready for use.

At this stage you will need the disc containing the program you wish to use.

Starting a Program

In order to use a program you should go through the following sequence:

1. Insert the disc in the disc drive with the label on top and towards you. Push it in fully and close the lid of the disc drive.
2. Hold down the SHIFT key and tap the BREAK key. The disc drive will whirr and after a wait of a few seconds either the program you require or a menu program will appear on the screen — this is called 'booting' a disc.
3. If this does not work check that the disc is inserted correctly and that you have carried out the 'boot' procedure correctly. If you still have difficulty either consult the chapter on Technical Tips or seek help from an expert.

Chip-based Software

Some of the more sophisticated programs for the BBC Micro are available on a micro-chip which can be plugged into a special socket inside the computer. These chips are normally referred to as ROMs. Once installed this program is instantly accessible once the computer is switched on and can be called up without using a disc by typing in a command beginning with an ⋆. For example, the word-processor PENDOWN can be called up by typing ⋆PD RETURN. The computer has space for only a limited number of such programs. The installation of ROMs into the computer requires care, and further advice is given in the chapter on Technical Tips. Again, if you are still unsure about doing the job, find an expert willing to do it for you.

Using a Program

It is important that you spend time familiarizing yourself with a program. Work your way through it using the instructions and advice provided with the program. Time spent at this stage will give you confidence when you start to use the program in the classroom. Plan carefully how best the program can be used and with which children. Bear in mind that the program may not be suitable for your needs and should, therefore, be kept for another occasion. The case studies and advice given in this book should be of help.

Finishing with a Program

There are a number of ways of exiting from a program. It is always advisable to leave a program by the correct means as explained in the instructions if this is possible. There are some programs which do not have an obvious way of finishing. If this is the case then there are a number of options you can follow. Try these methods, and if the first fails try the next until you are successful!

Exit by the documented method
Press ESCAPE
Press BREAK
Hold down CTRL and tap BREAK
Remove the disc and switch off the computer—this is guaranteed to work!

The Next Stage

Once you are confident in the use of discs for loading programs and are familiar with some straightforward examples of educational programs it is worth getting to grips with some of the more sophisticated types of program which involve storing, retrieving and printing out the children's work. Detailed discussion of the educational implications of such programs are dealt with elsewhere in this book.

If you are using a program such as a word-processor which requires you to save children's work for future use it is essential to ensure that you have a disc prepared to accept the information when you save it. This means you should have a blank, formatted disc ready to insert in the disc drive. The actual keys you will have to press will vary according to the program you are using but the process will be similar.

Saving Children's Work

1. Select the program option for saving children's work.
2. Insert the formatted disc in the disc drive. Many programs will prompt you to do this. The disc of the children's work may be called the 'work disc' or the 'data disc' and can be used by a class, a group or an individual according to the way you organize your discs.
3. Give the piece of work a name of seven letters or less and press RETURN. This will be the name under which it will be saved on the disc. It is worth making sure that it is a meaningful name and that you or the child involved keep a note of what the piece of work is called and which disc it is on — it can save a lot of searching of discs at a later date!

Retrieving Children's Work

Retrieving this work at a later date is simply the reverse of this process.

1. Select the program option for loading children's work.
2. Insert the appropriate work disc in the disc drive.
3. Type in the name of the piece of work you wish to load and press RETURN. This will load the piece of work into the computer's memory where it can be worked on or printed out.

Printing from the Computer

Many of the programs now available for the BBC Computer have the facility for printing out children's work or other information stored within the computer or on a disc. Programs which work in this way will have a command to initiate printing and while this will differ from one program to another the process used will be the same.

1. Ensure that there is paper in the printer.
2. Ensure that the printer is switched on.
3. Ensure that the printer is 'on line', that is, ready to print. This means that the coloured indicator light labelled 'on line' is on.
4. Carry out the procedure for printing which is specific to the program you are using.

There is further information on using printers in the chapter on Technical Tips.

The printer used for a project book cover

Conclusion

Using the computer in the primary school is, technically speaking, a relatively straightforward activity. If you have problems there are usually colleagues who can help and sometimes children who seem very able when it comes to sorting out problems with the computer. The real challenge for teachers presented by the presence of computers in primary schools is how to integrate their use into the classroom in a way that really enhances children's learning, and there are many suggestions about ways to achieve this in the following chapters.

3   The Early Years

Ann Snowdon

It is only in the last two years or so that a chapter concerned with the use of the micro in the Nursery and First School could have been feasible. The software was not available and teachers were reluctant to use the hardware with young children. Recently, however, interest has increased and more teachers appear to be asking for the Infant classes to be allocated computer time.

There are primarily two reasons for this: the increased quality of software and some newly available hardware has made the computer a more accessible tool for young children, and teachers have started questioning the belief that fourth year

The computer is an integral part of this nursery classroom

juniors are the youngest children capable of understanding the micro. Increasingly the computer is becoming as familiar in Nursery and Infant classes as the water tray and, if used successfully, the micro can offer another dimension to the children's learning, opening up a new world of first-hand experiences.

Organization

Which day of the week do you dread the most? Is it Monday, or the day you have P.E., or are you a victim of the new threat to your week — THE DAY YOU HAVE TO HAVE THE COMPUTER IN YOUR CLASS?.

The school organization which allocates the computer to each class for one day a week is not very satisfactory. It can become intrusive and dictate the curriculum instead of enhancing it, and there is the danger that the day becomes unnaturally divided into ten-minute slots so that all the children can have a turn, the program in use being a secondary issue. But within the constraints of this organization it is possible to use the computer more constructively, and the initial decision is which software to use. If this decision is made with reference to the overall scheme of work being covered by the children, then the 'computer day' will fit in with the rest of the children's activities. Instead of struggling to let every child have access each week, it is usually better to plan a much more long-term view where access to the computer happens at an appropriate moment in each child's learning and the experience is of value — whether it is for five minutes or an hour.

Ideally a teacher needs to know that the computer is available for a longer period. This obviously depends on the size of the school and the number of computers, and the length of time is usually a compromise between the ideal of, say, half a term, balanced against the time without a computer. For example in a school of six classes and one computer, is it better to have the computer once a year for half a term or twice a year for three weeks? The organization will vary from school to school and must be decided by each group of teachers. During the time a computer is in the classroom the teacher's planning can reflect that extra resource and the children have access to another dimension to their learning.

Language Development

(i) Reading

> We owe our young people a share of our reading
> pleasure, good books to make a reading dialogue a real
> experience and something that we can talk about
> together (Meek, 1982)

The computer has brought with it a new range of reading skills, and words such as 'boot', 'disc', etc., may now be recognized as part of a child's early sight vocabulary. Although the introduction of the computer into the classroom has added the need for 'screen reading' to the curriculum, we must be careful not to prematurely dismiss programs for a certain group of children due to the level of reading required. Software producers have come a long way in simplifying the route through a program, but inevitably a certain amount of reading is required, and this must be taken into consideration when planning the use of software.

Let us look at some pieces of software specifically designed to support children's reading. All of these programs aid the reading process through a 'whole language approach' where children's understanding of the whole story is used rather than separate letters or isolated words on a page. Pictures and text work together to give the children clues and cues to help them predict the meaning of text. It is important to include all types of literature in this work — both 'real stories' and structured reading schemes.

INFANT TRAY

This piece of software allows children to reveal a hidden text put in by the teacher. As it is context-free the teacher is able to construct any piece of text which meets the children's needs. Thus, a page from a reading scheme book could be entered, or the passage could relate to the current centre of interest in the classroom. This activity can be as simple as a single sentence with a few letters missing, or as complicated as a whole paragraph from *James and the Giant Peach*. By predicting letters, groups of letters or whole words, the children practise and extend their skills and, listening to the discussion between the group, the teacher is able to assess the children's understanding much more accurately than listening to them read.

```
One little frog has two eyes,
Four legs,
=n= m=u=h, no t=il,
==y= croak, croak =nd
Pl=p= in== =h= w====,
```

Use the ARROW keys to move,
Type your guess then press RETURN.

A partially completed text from INFANT TRAY

PROMPT/WRITER

This is a simple word-processing package which has combined two programs. It can be used with a concept keyboard (see Chapter 10), and it is through this that a teacher can make resources to support the teaching of reading. Overlays of pictures or pictures and text are revealed as text on the screen when the child presses the keyboard, and this text can then be printed out. This provides another illustration of how text relates to pictures, and of the one-to-one matching of the written and spoken word.

More sophisticated reading activities can be made using a combination of text on the screen and overlays or the conventional keyboard. Using the editing facilities the children can complete texts for cloze procedure activities, or fulfil other tasks related to text. The high quality of print makes this a valuable teacher resource for worksheets, etc., and children can also use the word-processing to build up a library of book reviews which are easily accessible.

Games for Inexperienced Readers

Teachers of Infant and Nursery classes are well aware of the many skills and concepts which appear to help in the complicated task of reading, and many of the activities designed to develop these skills and concepts are available when using the

○

MESU Primary Project
MESU Special Needs Software Centre
ⓒ **MESU 1987**

Filename: **SHOPS 1**

Artwork by Roy Outhwaite (MEP Low Attainers Project)
from program "SHOPS/SUPERMARKET (Northern Micromedia)

yoghurt	tea bags	toothpaste	toilet paper	soap	box	tin	bottle
butter	cheese	milk	coffee	lemonade	jar	bag	packet
margarine	fish fingers	lamb chop	sausages	hamburger	banana	onion	carrot
till	ice cream	buns	cake	bread	pear	apple	grapes

MESU *Keyboard Overlay* **PROMPT / WRITER**

computer. Whilst it might be claimed that the use of real materials is preferable to pictures on a screen, as the reading process is undoubtedly complex, any additional experience is likely to benefit some children. There are those children who seem to learn by osmosis, without any of the paraphernelia; others require many different activities and it could be that the computer will provide the key for some, perhaps simply in terms of motivation.

The design of these games is very familiar. Sequencing, matching and patterning are dealt with in programs such as BRICKS and CUBES, and these are very simple to use. They usually only require the use of the SPACEBAR and RETURN key, which means that very young children can successfully interact with the computer without adult supervision.

MOVING IN

A background story sets the scene and tells of a family who have moved to a new house. The screen shows a cross-section

I fell downstairs I had to go in an ambulance to hospital with Mummy and Daddy. I go in a bed with a broken leg .I had a operation I went home when I was better .

Simon Tudor

News using Prompt/Writer

of a house with kitchen, living room, bathroom, bedroom and attic, and the message:

'Tell me what to do.'

Using either a Concept Keyboard or typing at the conventional keyboard, the children can arrange the furniture in the house, for example:

'put a bath in the bathroom'
'put a cooker in the kitchen'
'put a piano in the living room'
'put Jim in the attic'
'make it cloudy'

Through dealing with a real situation (terraced house and flat versions are currently in preparation), the children work with sophisticated language structures as well as acquiring a useful sight vocabulary. There is a wealth of cross-curricular work possible with this piece of software, and many infant teachers have used the program as a starting point for projects on homes, buildings or families.

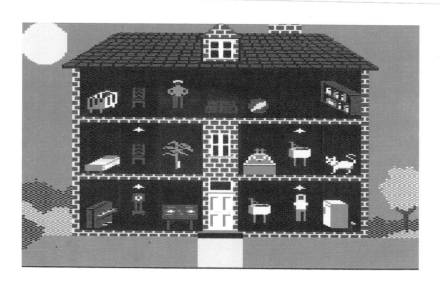

A colour printout of MOVING IN

(ii) Writing

Children want to write. They want to write the first day they attend school. This is no accident. Before they went to school they marked up walls, pavements, newspapers with crayons, chalk, pens or pencils ... anything that makes a mark. The child's marks say, 'I am'. (Donald Graves, 1983)

Helping children become writers is a part of language development which is tackled in a variety of ways in different schools.

Using MOVING IN as a base for a project on homes

Many questions surround the development of early writing skills. How should young children record their thoughts and feelings and how much emphasis should be placed on content and the process of writing? Whether you use the picture and sentence approach, sentence makers, printing or cursive, copying books or children's own attempts at text, the computer's ability in this area has added a new aspect to the development of children's writing.

Word-processing facilities mean that children now have access to a tool which removes the need for perfect pencil control. In every classroom there is the child who is full of ideas, who uses language with much creativity but when faced with that blank piece of paper awkwardly clutches a pencil, and is unable to record. A child once noticed the netball post through the window and said 'Look! The netball post looks like a straight finger pointing to the sky!' When asked to write his idea down he returned to the teacher with 'I like the netball post.'

The full use of word-processing can be a lengthy activity but lack of access time often means that the computer is used as the final draft tool for children's writing. Where possible this

The mouse's tale.
✱✱✱✱✱✱✱✱✱✱✱✱✱✱✱✱✱✱

Long,
   thin,
      soft,
    rubbery,
   smooth,
ticklish,
  droopy,
     sensitive,
   swift,
slippery,
   pointed.

(By Matthew Hurst.)

The computer has added a new aspect to children's writing

limited use as a 'copying out in neat' facility should be avoided. Apart from the DELETE capability a typewriter fulfils this role perfectly adequately. Saving pieces of writing would enable children to complete a piece of work on the computer over a longer period of time. Obviously some children might find it difficult to sustain the interest, but with additional input by the teacher at each stage it is possible to inspire young children to continue a piece of writing to its completion. Children can also work on partially written pieces of text put in by the teacher which allows the task to be shorter and also introduces the children to more sophisticated language.

Two pieces of software which are very suitable for use by nursery and infant children are PROMPT/WRITER and PENDOWN. The first has already been mentioned in relation to reading. PENDOWN is more sophisticated and offers the use of different fonts and a dictionary store. Both these programs can use the Concept Keyboard which automatically opens up word processing to the younger children, and the benefits of doing so are discussed in Chapter 4.

Another program which has been recently introduced is FAIRY TALES. This is a super package which enables very young children to make 'books' up to forty pages in length. They select from a library of pictures or 'character blocks' and enter text until they have completed a page to their own satisfaction. A further option is the use of picture characters which allows additional images to be made. Children respond remarkably enthusiastically to this activity and are keen to read each other's stories and to write stories with specific audiences in mind. This is another program which allows coloured print-outs if the appropriate printer is available. Black and white copies are however very effective and it is possible to save the stories on disc and then take them to a local teachers' centre or computer centre for printing.

(iii) Talking and Listening

So much masquerades under the disguise of 'discussion' which has no resemblance at all to human beings genuinely thrashing out a problem, pooling experience and speculating... There is an urgent need to explore new ways of working which will permit real talk... (James Britton, 1970)

Desk Top Publishing with
FAIRY TALES

The computer can be a powerful tool towards enhancing language development. Many programs encourage the children to talk to each other and make decisions, argue and think things through. It is vital that the computer is not seen as an isolated activity for one child. The value of children working together has been demonstrated to great effect in other areas of good practice in schools, and work with a computer is no exception. The hardware itself provides an excellent tool for studying the group dynamics between particular children. Do not be tempted to 'over-organize' a group of children assigned to the computer, as the skills they develop to accomplish their task are of great importance. The way that the children actually come to terms with the technology, how they organize their input to the computer — it is not unusual in a classroom to see children religiously changing seats to ensure everyone has a chance on the keyboard — are vital aspects of learning in the early years.

A topic folder for
GRANNY's GARDEN

One could take many pieces of software and assess their potential in terms of children's spoken language development. The role of the teacher is to organize the children's thoughts, help the group come to a decision and then assist them to rationalize what they have learned as a result of their actions, and the following two programs have particular qualities related to group discussion and the use of guided responses.

Play the game

I give up!
Please tell me your thing to wear.
Remember to type the/a/an/some
if you need to.

a hat.....................

The children have chosen an item which the computer does not identify. This prompts a request for the item to be named

Play the game

Type a question that would
pick out a hat
from trousers.

Do you wear it on your head?.....
....

Children can add the item to the SORTING GAME, but they must provide a suitable question

A partially revealed picture from WINDOW can prompt many questions: 'What is in the clown's left hand?', 'What is his dog doing?', etc

SORTING GAME

A simple decision tree game which is content-free. The children have to form questions which differentiate one item from another and can be answered with a yes or no. As the file grows the questions have to become more sophisticated.

WINDOW

This is a graphics package. The picture on the screen can be revealed in sections or continuously. The picture can be controlled through a Concept Keyboard or the QWERTY keyboard, and children can discuss and predict what they think the picture may be.

Mathematical Problem-Solving

Since we reported schools have introduced large numbers of microcomputers to their classrooms.... With the advent of the microcomputer it is much easier for a teacher to emphasise the practical applications of mathematics: for the microcomputer has made the applicability of mathematics in everyday life manifest. (W. Cockcroft, 1985).

(i) Turtle Graphics

Many Infant and Nursery Schools have become involved with LOGO since the appearance of various floor Turtles. Usually children begin by using a programmable toy such as BIG TRAK. Unfortunately this was taken off the market, but a new controllable robot ROAMER has very recently been launched and promises to be an exciting development in the use of logo-type languages for young children. As David Griffiths and Howard Gillings describe in Chapter 9, the children can then go on to use Floor Turtles, such as the Valiant, and progress to the use of a screen turtle.

The use of a screen Turtle with a program such as DELTA is more accessible to 3- to 8-year olds through the use of Concept Keyboard overlays. Manipulating backward and forward movements and 90-degree turns are suitable beginnings encouraging the children to think carefully about distance and make comparisons. Later the constraints can be taken away and children can be encouraged to experiment with different angles.

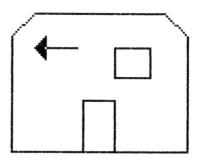

Drawing with DELTA

(ii) Games

There are some computer programs which take on the 'game' format. These are a challenge in themselves but the real value is the discussion and investigation required for the children to discover *how* to 'win' the game.' Some quality examples of this type of software are:

COLONY: a two-player game which may also be played against the computer, involving acquiring possession of all the cells.

STRATEGY: the familiar noughts and crosses game on different grids.

FROGS: a problem involving two sets of frogs which have to change places within certain movement constraints.

XOR: an arcade maze game which only allows a limited number of moves and graduates in difficulty. It also has an option for children to design their own mazes.

All of these programs set the children a problem to solve. Some of them provide help facilities, but the educational value is to be found in the thought processes involved in solving the problem and not merely getting the answer right.

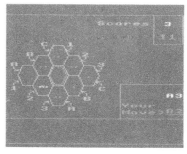

Purple is about to 'colonize' yellow and win the game (COLONY)

(iii) Information Handling

The work that children in nursery and infant schools engage in often involves collecting large amounts of information and the computer is an ideal tool for storing and handling such data. It is advisable to introduce this facility using the knitting needle and punch card method where a file comprises all the punched cards, each card representing a record and the slots and holes representing the different fields. This arrangement corresponds to a computer data-handling program, and the punch cards give the children a concrete example of the structure of such a program.

Perhaps the most appropriate piece of software available which provides a simple introduction to presenting information in an easily interpreted graphical form is DATASHOW. This enables the results of simple numerical surveys to be entered

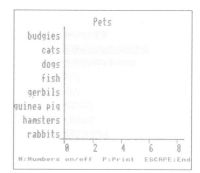

The screen picture of a histogram from DATASHOW can be printed out in black and white

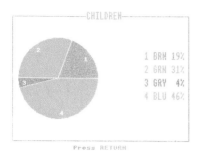

Instant pie-charts can be made and printed out using OURFACTS

into the computer and a histogram or pie chart to be produced on screen and printed out.

Next in order of sophistication is OURFACTS (a combination of OURSELVES and FACTFILE). The children can create and, perhaps most importantly of all, interrogate files of information on any subject. Again, files can be displayed in the form of a count graph, cumulative count and scattergram, and all the information can be printed out in columns of text.

These programs are easily integrated into the mathematical investigations tackled by young children, and a group of children will often work on a problem set by a piece of computer software alongside other children using multi-base or logiblocs.

Mike Matson's introduction to his stories about friends ... and the friend he created for WORLD WITHOUT WORDS

The three stories in this book are about **friends.** Not the sort of friends that you and I normally think of, but friends just the same. I expect that when you are with your friends you spend a lot of time talking to each other. Have you ever thought about what it would be like to have a friend who came from another world, a friend who couldn't speak your language, a friend who wasn't human, or a friend who just can't see or hear or talk? I often think that when you have a **real** friend you don't need to talk anyway. Just being with your friend is enough.

One of the stories, **Fuff,** came to me one afternoon in winter when I was sitting on a rocky beach. There was no-one else to be seen and I began to imagine what it would be like if it was the end of the world and I was the last person alive. I decided that if I was to survive on my own I would have to make some friends. Not 'make friends' by finding someone but 'make friends' by making them in my head. I wonder if that's what you do.

I hope you enjoy the stories.

Mike Matson

Creativity

>...if giving them 'words and no pictures' gets imaginations working what will happen if they get nothing but pictures? No words. Worlds without words. I've done my bit: now it's all down to you. (Mike Matson, 1988)

(i) Adventures and Simulations

This genre of computer software is dealt with in more detail in another chapter; however, it would be impossible to discuss the education of young children without mentioning fantasy and role-play.

Both these types of software — one a parallel of the real world, the other a fictitious world — open new doors to a realm of first-hand experiences which can enhance children's learning across the curriculum. Any teacher contemplating using such a piece of software must be aware of the planning involved. If you believe the work can only be carried out via the keyboard and that the main aim is to get to the end as quickly as possible, then the value of the software is reduced considerably. To enter the worlds of Dragons, Spaceships, Wizards and those Without Words means incorporating all aspects of the curriculum to enrich the children's experience.

GRANNY'S GARDEN: one of the earliest successful adventure games produced by Mike Matson. When the children visit their Granny they find the garden (like the wardrobe to Narnia) is a gateway to the Kingdom of the Mountains. Here they are requested to help the raven rescue the King and Queen and find their children.

DRAGON WORLD: a follow-up to GRANNY'S GARDEN where the world of the baby dragons is explored. The adventure is again in two parts and the children discover the importance of real treasures. The ways in which the theme of treasures can be developed whilst using this program is discussed by Monica Hughes in Chapter 5.

THE TEACHER'S CUPBOARD: adventures begin as the children walk through the door of the teacher's cupboard. They meet enchanted animals and are transported to a magical land where they have to complete tasks and puzzles.

INFANT FARMER: the children are given the opportunity to wander around a farm and they are able to 'feed' the animals, herd the cows and bring the duck home.

(ii) Art and Music

When teaching the skills involved in these two areas of the curriculum many teachers will claim 'I'm not musical', or 'I'm not very good at drawing.' There are programs available now which will encourage those teachers to explore art and music, as well as provide another resource to those who have already achieved a great deal with their children.

> Music is a universal language for communicating and expressing emotions. It can bring pleasure and satisfaction to those involved in it. With the help of technology it can be accessible to those with little or no musical training and can also bring success to children... (Andy Pierson, 1988).

Although both the following programs are discussed in detail in later chapters it is worth emphasizing that young children can quite easily use them. This is certainly illustrated by the examples of work which very young children have produced using IMAGE.

COMPOSE: this program provides a graphic musical environment in which children can create their own compositions. There are several files of nine pictures — each picture has its own melody — and these can be put together to build a tune. Before long the children become familiar with the sounds that go with each picture and make decisions about which are pleasant together. They can go on to create their own melodies by experimenting with musical building blocks. Any tune created by the children can be played by the computer at different speeds, and can be accompanied by conventional instruments. Although very few computer keys are involved when using the program, Chris Hopkins has designed a concept keyboard overlay which make the program accessible to the youngest of children (see Chapter 10).

IMAGE: This is another example of a sophisticated and powerful program which is immediately accessible to young children by the provision of a 'Mouse'. This enables children to interact with the computer without having to touch the keyboard, and has obvious advantages for young children and those with fine motor problems. Using the mouse to move around the screen and operate their commands, the children can create displays involving shape, line, texture and pattern. Text can be built up and areas can be repeated, distorted, rotated and rearranged. Perhaps most exciting of all, video images can be transferred to the screen and used in the work. The finished picture can then be printed or stored on disc for subsequent display. All this may sound frighteningly technical but the beauty of it is that young children's own creativity and willing-ness to experiment releases them from any inhibitions and enables them to create with ease (see Chapter 12 for examples).

Conclusion

It would be difficult to disagree with the view that education in the early years is one of the hardest, most exciting and most rewarding tasks faced by teachers. Understanding what is going on in a young child's mind and what concepts are thoroughly understood is a complex matter. It involves close observations and many different approaches to the curriculum content. Teachers constantly apply themselves to the task of sorting and sifting through equipment and resources, seeking out those things which not only enrich children's experience but also provide useful insight and evidence of a child's development so that the next appropriate step may be planned.

Undoubtedly, the education of young children should be founded on first-hand experience. A few years ago the com-puter was not offering the teacher of such children anything with which to extend the curriculum already on offer. Now, there is a vast amount of software from which to choose. The teacher's role is to evaluate the recommended programs and only use those which offer an additional resource which enhances their learning and matches, if not betters, the rich and imaginative activities already presented to children at school in their early years.

The advent of the micro in schools was looked upon with some scepticism by many teachers but the growing availability of quality software has increased the demands on publishers for more and better quality programs. Let us hope that the unrival-led expertise which exists in this country will continue to be used in the production of materials which so enrich the quality of classroom experience.

Programs Mentioned

Colony
Compose
Datashow
Delta
Dragon World
Fairy Tales
Frogs
Granny's Garden
Image
Infant Tray
Infant Farmer
Moving In
Ourfacts
Pendown
Prompt/Writer
Sorting Game
The Teacher's Cupboard
Strategy
Window
World Without Words
Xor

References

Britton, J. (1970) *Language and Learning*, Harmondsworth, Penguin.
Cockcroft, W. (1985) 'Does mathematics still count?' in *New Scientist*, 9 May, London, New Science Publications.
Graves, D. (1983) *Writing: Teachers and Children at Work*, London, Heinemann.
Matson, M. (1988) *World Without Words*, Barnstaple, 4Mation.
Meek, M. (1982) *Learning to Read*, London, Bodley Head.
Microelectronics in Education Project (1985) *Infant and First Schools: The Role of the Microcomputer*, MEP.
Pierson, A. (1988) 'Who says you're not musical?', in *Key Ideas* 1, 1, Judgevalid Ltd.
Schools Council (1985) *The Practical Curriculum*, London, HMSO.

4 Language

Philip Mann

It is but a few years since computers were considered solely as number-crunching machines. This was indeed what they were initially devised for: handling vast amounts of numbers, solving equations and solving numerical problems.

Within our homes and classrooms we now have computers which are more concerned with language or text handling than coping with numbers. Modern computers demonstrate that they are just as capable of handling words as they are numbers, and suddenly every office has a word-processor as part of its furniture. The paperless office is a reality and the new technology allows us to write at the keyboard and send our text round the world in seconds using modems or Fax machines. There is in our midst a most potent purveyor and transporter of words.

If I may take you back five years...

Tony was a child in my class with learning difficulties. He had a short attention span and a poor self image. He seemed ham-fisted, and always wanted to start a piece of work again. But when he saw the challenge of the adventure game he became a different child.

I had set up in my class an early adventure game, no colourful graphics or clever sound effects, merely words on the flickering screen. For days Tony glowered at the old TV set we used as a monitor, he read the state of play within the adventure game, he tried the options, he talked out loud, he deduced, he reasoned, he asked and he swore. For the first time whilst he had been in my class the words on the screen had transported him to a micro-world where he had risen to the challenge. As time progressed he gradually inched his way to victory. Whenever his half hour was up he would return to his desk with a different light in his eye, saying that he had the torch, the Barclaycard, the ladder, the axe and whatever else was necessary to reach his goal, and that surely it wouldn't be long now before victory — and that he would be the first.

A matter of days later during an after-school session he

'I've got the torch, Barclaycard and the ladder'

He dashed down the corridor truly victorious

reached the end of the adventure game and this was a time of mixed blessings for me. The cries and whoops were music to my ears, he radiated success, he dashed down the corridor truly victorious. What amazed me was the unstinting attention he had paid to this rather frivolous enterprise and, more particularly, the relish with which he pondered the clues using his undoubted capacity for logical reasoning which had been hitherto unawoken. Here was something that he had talked about with enthusiasm — something that spurred him into action and with his 'streetwise' capacity had made him manipulate the clues and strive for success. Somehow my workcards and creative writing stimuli paled into insignificance against this potent purveyor and transporter of words!

This incident demonstrates the power that computers can have and how a piece of software such as an adventure game can unlock potential within a child — potential to exploit language in its various forms.

The Learning of Language

Language transcends so much of the learning process. 'Man interposes a network of words between the world and himself, and thereby becomes the master of the world' (Georges Gusdorf, 1975). The development of this network of words is a complicated and fascinating process but not within the scope of this book. Nevertheless the acquisition of language is by far the most important aspect of the learning process. This separates us from the animals as we become symbol-using creatures by our ability to make symbolic representations of the world around us through the use of words — first spoken then written.

The child who can listen well and has learned to articulate clearly is at an advantage when the more complex skills — reading and writing — come to be learned. Early writing tends to be expressive and retains a close affinity to speech. 'To begin to write is to put to a new use those linguistic resources that have so far been developed entirely by speaking and listening' (Bullock Report, 1975).

The wonder of learning to read is that it is still so much a mysterious process. Through the history of man's learning 'there is no one method, medium, approach, device or philosophy that holds the key to the process of learning to read' (Bullock Report, 1975). A delicate balance has to be maintained between the emphasis on the mechanics of reading (phonetics and the converting of symbols into sounds) and keeping a child's interest alive by reading for pure pleasure. Again it seems that the child who has had a good early exposure to the spoken word and who is able to talk adequately is at an advantage when learning to read.

The four areas LISTENING, TALKING, READING and WRITING are intertwined in a complex manner and appear to depend on and develop from one another. 'No single mode of language is more important than any other since all are needed for effective communication, and by implication, for effective learning' (Wallen, 1988).

The Computer as Teaching Resource

Any classroom resource which allows the teacher or child to use the medium of language in whatever form, is going to benefit the acquisition of language. A linguistically rich environment should be colourful, stimulating, challenging and fun. The classroom-based computer can offer just such opportunities to enhance the language environment. Wherever listening, talking, reading and writing happen then the computer with relevant software may add to the child's educational environment in an unrivalled manner.

The Essence of Computing : Software

The software which enhances language is forever changing. During the years that counties have standardized on hardware there has been a continuous improvement in primary software. Programmers have learned that it is better to work in close contact with teachers and to pilot their work carefully before releasing it onto the educational market. This programmer/teacher partnership produces software of high educational credibility. How much a piece of software can be utilized within the curriculum is limited only by the expertise of the individual teacher. I have seen a particular program produce little educational benefit within a certain class, little cross-curricular development and minimum excitement: the same program handled in a different way by a teacher with more enthusiasm or motivation produced exciting results and benefitted the children in a positive way. Most probably the former teacher would achieve minimal results whatever extra resources were employed, while the latter teacher could most likely achieve an exciting working environment with a minimum of resources. In many cases how the computer is used with a particular piece of software is very much up to the individual teacher's professional abilities and their willingness to exploit any resource.

It is difficult to categorize software into specific language areas. However, examples will be given which will demonstrate the supportive nature of pieces of software of the four elements of language, namely listening, talking, reading and writing.

Listening and Talking

Listening and talking inevitably go together, so let us look at the classroom computer situations which will facilitate and promote such activities. Much of the software in question is suitable for a small group of pupils, preferably up to three or four, to be working at the keyboard at one time, and by having such groups at the computer keyboard, discussion at various levels invariably takes place. Apart from the software designed for small group activity, there are programs which are aimed at class discussion around the computer, where the teacher encourages discussion and decision-making amongst the pupils. The adventure game scenario is a marvellous example of this, and although such programs are covered by another chapter in this book, the importance of the adventure game cannot go unmentioned whilst focusing on language.

Most adventure games are designed to be worked at by small groups of pupils moving at their own pace through the adventure in the normal classroom situation, and there will be times also when the whole class will be involved sitting together round the micro as the teacher explains a certain part of the adventure or demonstrates some areas of difficulty encountered by the children. The careful teacher may exploit this opportunity so that, rather than direct answers being given to difficulties encountered, gradually, by discussion and shared experience, a mutually agreed solution is forthcoming.

The adventure game can generate a whole micro-world of exciting places, people or characters, situations and challenges. Entering the exact words via the keyboard is often essential in order to succeed in an adventure game, so the child learns the importance of verbal accuracy — this accuracy being the culmination of discussion, i.e., listening and talking.

One of 52 Podd Activity sheets

Although a huge variety of programs exist, covering a wide range of subjects, one thing the majority have in common is the generation of discussion. Some programs have been designed specifically for this purpose however, and an example of this is STORY STARTS. Screens of text accompanied by graphical illustrations are read out by teachers or pupils and at the end of the page a choice is offered of three possible directions. Following discussion a democratic decision is made and a direction selected, revealing a different scenario and a further set of choices. The stories never actually finish, and the children are left in a cliff-hanging situation offering the opportunity for some creative written work.

Perhaps one of the most endearing characters of the monitor screen is PODD. This tomato-like character has been invented in order to search the action words within children's vocabulary. Podd is capable of doing about 120 actions. When a child enters at the keyboard (correctly spelled) an action that Podd is capable of doing then he will proceed to carry it out. These actions are as diverse as gliding, sneezing, blushing and vanishing. There is a synonym structure to the program which allows children to think of similar action words — walk, step, stride and pace for example. Obviously designed for infant-aged pupils, Podd can remain stimulus material for much older children, and the possibilities for Podd micro-worlds are boundless. Whole generations of Podds, their life style and habitat, are all open to the initiative of the teacher and the imagination of the children. A Podd Pack has been produced (Doherty, 1987) which provides freely copyable A4 material which can be used to enhance language and number activities.

STORYLINE is a simple program designed as a stimulus for creative writing or drama but is also most useful as a stimulus to class discussion. The program structure is such that there are three variables — character, action and place. Teachers may write their own variables for inclusion in the program, and the sequence of variables is then randomly generated and the result displayed on the screen or put out to the printer. For example,

Three old ladies riding bicycles through a mountain pass.
A fat chimney sweep eating strawberries at the bottom of the sea.
Several tall policemen clapping loudly in the market.

These bizarre situations amuse the children and prompt explanation. There is opportunity for some really imaginative discussion to take place around this program with children of primary age.

Similar to the above program is WORDPLAY. This generates words at random placing them within a phrase but the teacher or child has control over the form which the phrases take. The program requires the operator to set up the phrase form and to know what nouns, verbs, adjectives and adverbs are. For example the phrase form may be set to this pattern:

noun, adjective noun verb adverb, verb

Vocabulary is also entered under the appropriate part of speech catagory: hence the above phrase pattern may be generated as follows:

Autumn, brown leaves turning crisply, falling

or:

Branches, hot earth floating loudly, vanishing

Several lines of phrases thus generated may appear on the screen and meaningful material may be printed out or saved to disc. There is more of a chance that such generated material is unacceptable and usually after several runs something of an acceptable quality is produced. The important aspect is for the children to decide what makes the material acceptable: to discuss why a particular phrase is unsuitable.

This program has two levels. If the teacher sets up the phrase structure then obviously the children do not need to know the parts of speech used within the program. However the children can certainly participate in the compiling of the lists of the various parts of speech, an important exercise in itself. There then comes the acceptance of the generated poem. Is it suitable and does it make sense?

A deeper level of involvement is the additional aspect of the children actually determining the phrase structure by entering the particular parts of speech at the appropriate stage of the program. This program can offer opportunity to a wide range of primary-aged children and, unusually perhaps, combines elements of language structure with creativity, neatly satisfying two demands of the Kingman Report (DES, 1988). Once again the relevant point here is the discussion element available through this program, although, as with so many of these programs, there are other important language opportunities within it, especially for writing.

Reading

So much of pupil-computer interaction consists of reading the on-screen situation. This includes menus, prompt lines and instructions, and most of the software mentioned in the last section on talking and listening is relevant in this section. Once the teacher has progressed into the program with a group of children or the whole class, demonstrating the possibilities and pitfalls, the pupils are eager to go ahead by themselves and so will have to read the screen in order to progress. Screen characters are rarely similar to the print style of real books or reading schemes; however, as with the seven-segment numerals we have all come to accept on our digital watches and elsewhere, children seem to accommodate the diversity of characters quickly.

Some children can read perfectly and annunicate accurately and yet find it difficult to be articulate about what they have just read. The skill involves listening internally to what they are reading and remembering the content of what is read, and the traditional classroom activity of English Comprehension hopes to develop just such a skill through the appreciation of context and deductions made from contextual clues.

One of the most taxing pieces of software which relies heavily on contextual and syntactical clues is DEVELOPING TRAY. Here a piece of text is made to appear on the screen with some or all the letters of the alphabet excluded. If all the letters are excluded then it is only the punctuation marks within the text which appear.

```
------------------------------------------------

====  ==  ju== = ==mpl= ==x= ==  === ==w
===  ==w v====== =f ===y w==k=.
= ====k == == = v==y =xc====q
p==q==m, ==d ='m l==k==q f==w==d ==
m=k==q ==x== == = w==d p==c===== =uc=
==  P== D=w=.

------------------------------------------------
```

A printout of a DEVELOPING TRAY text

The aim of this program is to insert all the correct letters thus finishing with a piece of completed text. There is a scoring system which increases or decreases according to the success or failure of the pupil. For example pupils may buy letters, reducing their score by ten points, and make predictions, when each correctly spelled letter adds to the score. An incorrectly predicted letter deducts two from the running total, and bonus points are given for predictions longer than a single letter. The final Grand Total is given by the 'jackpot' multiplied by the score.

There is a definite strategy for success in this game. It is interesting to see which children discover these strategies first. Something akin to 'contextual blindness' can occur where children will see that a five-letter word is there in the text yet they are so blinkered by what they think should fit in that they will attempt to insert words of six letters or more!

This program may be used at different levels within the classroom, for example as a deluxe cloze procedure. When this program is used in conjunction with a piece of text from an on-going theme or topic then it can serve as a real test in the understanding of certain chosen details, and teachers may make up any number of 'hidden' texts for the children to develop.

Once again careful choice of who works with whom is important. Much will be gained from discussion at the keyboard, but it is sensible to have pupils of similar reading age working together.

Adults and children are often surprised at how little graphical information is necessary to make intelligent and successful predictions. It reveals the true nature of reading: 'not barking at print but playing a psycho-linguistic guessing game' (Shenk, 1985).

This powerful program demonstrates clearly the value of discussing, anticipating, predicting, hypothesizing and testing from contextual clues. The autor of this program, Bob Moy, originally considered its use to be with secondary pupils who were struggling with their reading. He comments, 'Children who had been drowning in the shallow end of their lives suddenly found out that they could swim if they were plunged into the deep end' (Moy, 1986). However, it was quickly realized that this program was suitable for many different groups of children. A version for younger children, INFANT TRAY, has been devised, which is very similar in structure but without the complex scoring system, and with double-sized characters on the screen. In contrast, the program has been used successfully by A level students whilst exploring Shakespearean texts.

Writing

A child in primary school may well spend more time in activities connected with writing than anything else. 'Writing has always been accorded a high prestige in our educational system, and this is due in large part to its traditional use as a means by which students put on record what they learned' (Bullock Report, 1975). This skill could be considered the 'blossom on the language tree', where the roots are the listening and talking skills and the trunk and branches the skill of reading. Much of the child's time is spent in the acquisition of the physical skills of pencil manipulation, handwriting style and page layout, and apart from these demanding skills there are the additional requirements of vocabulary, spelling, punctuation and logical sentence construction. It may not surprise us that so much time is indeed spent in this demanding area of a child's education. One feature of the growing 'Children as Writers' movement is the emphasis on writing as a craft which can be learned by doing. 'Now we can recognize what a major step forward this (the focus on the writing process) was, to begin to think how children can be helped and encouraged to compose, transcribe, review and possibly redraft for a range of purposes' (Roger Beard, 1988). Thus, children are increasingly given opportunities to explore and develop their ideas, to draft, redraft and publish and this approach has fortunately coincided with the arrival of word-processing programs within our classrooms. A minor revolution in the acquisition of writing skills has thus begun. 'The computer has the power to affect profoundly the way every writer works ... by removing a major barrier that stands between writers and their words: the labour of getting words onto paper' (Hammond, 1984).

It should be stated clearly here that the author is not propounding the idea that all traditional methods of teaching writing skills are to be thrown overboard. The introduction of word-processing in the classroom can comfortably fit alongside these conventional approaches. The strength of word-processing lies in its ability to liberate the child from the physical constraints connected with the mechanics of putting words onto paper and the flexibility connected with such programs has some profound effects on many aspects of writing. Of course the importance of training children in an acceptable handwriting style, the teaching of punctuation, spelling, and indeed all the surface features, remains. Peter Hunter (1988) has provided a useful diagram which summarizes two hierarchies: those concerned with text, and those concerned with skills.

Alongside the textual hierarchy is a hierarchy of concerns. At the highest level, where the focus of attention is on the book as a whole, the important concerns are to do with the writer's intention in writing the book.... At the word level, spelling enters the scene and, at this and lower levels, concerns about handwriting loom large... What the hierarchy of concerns does is to draw attention to those skills, which relate to particular levels in the hierarchy, and to the fact that many of them have to be developed, it would seem, together. (Peter Hunter, 1988)

Textual	*Typical Concerns/Skills*			
BOOK	Overall intention, plan, plot, structure of book.	↑	↑	↑
CHAPTER	Sub-plot, contribution to book, development of particular theme or aspect, chapter plan.	Global	Composition	Semantic
PARAGRAPH	Elucidation of a particular idea, character description, scene or location, part of dialogue, contribution to chapter, relation with neighbouring paragraphs.			
SENTENCE	Contribution to paragraph, links with neighbouring sentences, length, structure, grammar, punctuation, choice of vocabulary.	Local	Transcription	Syntactic
WORD	Choice of word, place in sentence, spelling, punctuation.			
LETTER	Spelling, handwriting.			
STROKE	Handwriting, size, pressure, angle, speed.	↓	↓	↓

A Hierarchy of Concerns in Writing

The word-processor is more than a glorified typewriter. Conventional typewriters write forwards and correcting or manipulating text is difficult or impossible. The power of the word-processor lies in its ability to hold text in a state of limbo, for the user to be able to manipulate the text until the end result is achieved and then commit the text to paper. A pupil commented 'You don't write anything until it's finished.' (Murray, 1988).

The ability to re-draft in a manner which is most difficult and time-consuming in the conventional manner is simplicity itself with the word-processor.

> The teacher's first response to a piece of writing should be personal and positive... . Correction and revision are of unquestionable value. The best approach is for the teacher to go over the pupil's work, discussing persistent errors, suggesting solutions where the writing has

run into difficulties, and talking over alternative ways of phrasing something. In much of the writing that takes place in school the pupil's first attempt is expected to be the finished article; there is not enough encouragement of the idea of a first draft to be followed by a second more refined production. (Bullock Report, 1975).

Mark, bright and articulate, but a poor reader, produced this first draft

The word-processor is designed to allow as much correction, re-phrasing and editing as is necessary, and the child can learn the importance of working on a piece of text, possibly over several days, before accepting the final draft. An extremely useful, practical guide to this approach can be found in *Writers' Workshop* by Gregory, Lyons and Redfern (1988):

Part of writing development is the increasing recognition on the part of the writer of what needs to be done for the writing to accomplish its purpose. For this to happen, children need to be able to work on a piece of writing over extended periods of time. Writer's Workshop creates opportunities for drafting and revising, for consultation and discussion with the teacher and other children, and for self-editing and publishing. Access to word processing facilities can make a real difference to the children's willingness to work on a piece of writing, both at the redrafting and at the editing stage.

```
THE PARK IN THE DARK
Shadows crept across the misty park.
A barn owl in a nearby tree. Hoot! It
went hoot, hoot! It was hunting for
food. I swivelled round like a
corkscrew just in time to see it catch
a mouse and soar into the dark.  It
was dawn and I could hardly see a
thing.  I felt I was being followed
but there was nobody there.  I looked
up and there up in the tree was a
sparrow making a nest between the
branches. But suddenly a figure, about
the size of a small dog, appeared just
ahead of me.  As I stared through the
poor light, I could just make out a
fox running from one side of the road
to the other. I felt cold, not just
because of the snow, but with the
lonliness too. Then I saw my home! I
soon forgot about the snow and before
I knew it, I was in my home drinking
cocoa.
                Mark
```

PROMPT|WRITER enabled Mark to produce this final version. 'That's blooming marvellous!' he said

Word-processor Organization

The choice of work-processing program is dependent upon the age and sophistication of the child. There are programs designed for infant-aged pupils, these being straightforward packages which are user-friendly and not sophisticated. Further up the age range it makes perfect sense for the older more able child to learn to use the more office-oriented system. Basically all word-processors do the same: allow the manipulation of text on the screen and print out the result. The degree of complexity is then determined by the additional facilities available: the amount of text stored, the inclusion of spelling checks and the ability to print in different fonts for example. Perhaps a quick run through the main options would help the reader at this stage.

Amber had to go to the hospital because she had a sprained ankle but she didn't go in an ambulance. Mummy took her into the hospital and Mummy stayed there in the hospital and Daddy was at work . Mummy bought me some powder .

Laila Clarke.

A simple word-processing program can add a new dimension to an infant's news

WRITER has been a most popular word-processor package, simple to use, disc-based and providing the opportunity for teachers to set up options in formatting and print size. This package has now been superceded by the more versatile PROMPT/WRITER which is the amalgamation of WRITER and another word-processing package called PROMPT. The advantage with this one is the better choice of fonts and formatting.

PENDOWN has been designed for a wide ability range, and offers more than just a word-processing system. It includes a dictionary facility, a text planning facility and the means whereby children may design their own fonts (typefaces) or edit existing ones. The PENDOWN manual is excellent and contains many suggestions for using the program. Since its release there have been several supplementary discs offering yet more fonts and something called SIGNWRITER. This is marvellous for printing out labels for displays, a must for any classroom.

FOLIO, another disc system, offers a number of formatting options and many fonts to choose from. Perhaps not as user-friendly as those mentioned above, FOLIO has however become popular in many schools. More versatile systems such as WORDWISE PLUS and INTERWORD certainly have their place with the experienced young word-processor user. These two systems have been designed for office use but would form a logical progression from those systems previously mentioned. With these two ROM-based systems spelling-checking is available, an important feature that pupils should have experience

BROADWAY

SMILE

HOLIDAY

JUPITER

FLEUR

0123456789

PENDOWN fonts

with when they have progressed away from the more basic systems.

An important factor when using word-processing with children who have no keyboard skills is the time taken to achieve text on the screen. The pupil will inevitably spend a great deal of time searching for the appropriate keys. This results in teacher and pupil frustration. There is the added complication that the symbols on the keys are in upper case (capitals), whilst the young writer will most likely be only used to lower-case lettering. Rather than stick little labels on the keyboard, the teacher should regard this as a marvellous opportunity for children to come to terms with the fact that all letters do indeed have two shapes!

Most of the word-processors for young pupils have a Concept Keyboard option; these will help circumnavigate the upper/lower case problem. The teacher is able to replace the standard keyboard with Concept Keyboard and lower-case overlay. It is also possible to change the order of letters (away from the anachronistic QWERTY system), or indeed replace

MESU Primary Project
MESU Special Needs Software Centre
© MESU 1987

Filename: **PHRASE 2**

mum	dad	television		am	is	was		
home	house			were	will	can	go
shop	day			have	has	come	went
car	park			saw	got	get	
I	my	me	you	our	the	like	play	look
it	we	he	him	some	a			
with	not	out	in	to	.	CAPITAL	RETURN	←	→
and	no	yes	of	s	?	SPACE	DELETE	↑	↓

MESU *Keyboard Overlay* PROMPT / WRITER

letters with complete words. This latter system allows children who are having real difficulties to produce a piece of written work built up from complete words.

The Concept Keyboard is a powerful addition to the hardware of any classroom but especially to the infant classroom or when teaching children with motor control difficulties. The board may be placed on the floor well away from the computer but kept within sight of the monitor and many overlays can be prepared which are suitable for certain groups of children or individual children. Further uses of this piece of hardware are explained in Chapter 10 (*Beyond the QWERTY Keyboard*).

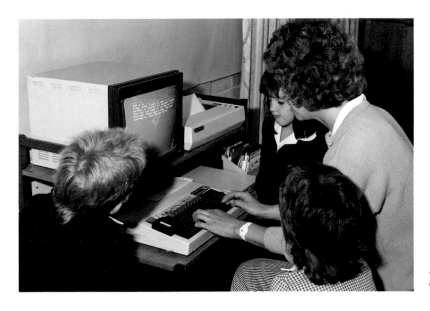

An adult can occasionally speed up the process of re-drafting

To speed up the input of text at the keyboard, an adult or older child may sit at the computer whilst the pupil(s) dictate the text. There is the organizational problem of resourcing such a keyboard operator but the possibility of parental help should not be overlooked.

Here we arrive at an interesting educational discussion point. The vocabulary forthcoming when this organization is used is invariably much richer. The children, released from the burden of the physical process of putting pencil to paper or even having to think about the spelling, are now able to give full rein to their creative processes. Story writing ceases to be the piecemeal, laboured process involving conventional pencil and paper (and rubber!). Their creative thoughts, their reporting of enquiry, their newspaper article, can be magically placed onto paper, displayed on the wall, published in book form or indeed taken home as an example of their day's efforts.

As the pupil's writing skills improve then the dependence on a helper at the keyboard should diminish. Appropriate spellings may be made available at the top of their text which the pupil can scroll up to when required. A previously saved file with such spellings available may be loaded into the word-processor at the top of their page and when no longer required deleted from the text prior to being printed.

Rather than having just vocabulary available at the top of the page it would be possible to load in the beginning or end of a story, the task being for the pupil to complete the story.

Listening to a group of two or three pupils sitting round the computer whilst they discuss the relative merits of particular vocabulary is fascinating, and not so easily set up in the more conventional classroom writing situations.

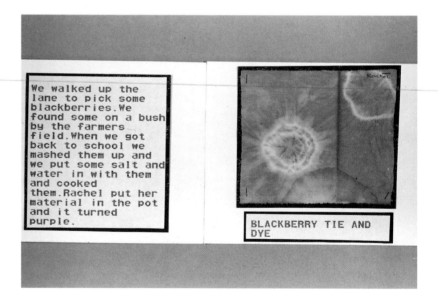

Topic work with PENDOWN

Desk-Top Publishing

There is a blurred dividing line between a word-processing program or package and what is known as desk-top publishing programs, DTP for short. Having a word-processing package, printer and photocopying facilities allows the setting up of a simple publishing system. The phrase 'desk-top publishing' is a popular title which describes just such a simple system. Pupils and teachers, through the use of appropriate software, can go into newspaper or newsletter publications, produce program-mes for concerts, notices, posters. Indeed there are limitless opportunities for publication both within class and within school administration. Any word-processing program may be used for desk-top publishing provided pupils or teachers are prepared to cut and paste the text produced and lay out the text to the desired format, then photocopy. A DTP program gives added facilities to do such cutting, pasting and formatting on the screen prior to printing. DTP packages are designed to make the production of the required document as smooth as possible. They usually allow the insertion of graphics and the insertion of text around these graphics whilst on the screen. Graphics may be loaded from a library of pictures on disc or may be drawn on the screen and later inserted into the text.

A superbly effective program which can be used to enhance children's writing is CAPTION which provides a graphical framework for poems or short pieces of prose. This can be used by children of all ages and can be a powerful motivator for those children who struggle to write more than a few words at a time. Print-outs can be made in black and white, but the use of a colour printer has a dramatic impact on the finished product.

... just as though they were in a real newsroom

FRONT PAGE EXTRA and TYPESETTER! are two DTP programs which are at the lower end of sophistication. These programs emulate the newspaper format and so give teachers the opportunity to research the style of journalists and the whole process of newspaper compilation and production. FRONT PAGE EXTRA is easy to use and prints out a crisp newspaper-like page which will thrill any child. There is the opportunity to leave blank frames on the pages in order to paste on photos or drawings at a later date. An example of this can be found in Chapter 7. TYPESETTER! is a more sophisticated word-processing package more within the realm of desk-top publishing, in which, again, empty frames may be used to insert graphics after printing out the page. The program is constructed so that the pupil goes from editing department to the printing room just as though they were in a real newspaper printing house.

AMX PAGEMAKER and FLEET STREET EDITOR are more advanced examples of DTP packages and although not for normal primary use, they may well have a place in schools to aid the production of booklets or worksheets. Both these packages can manipulate graphics and text.

Published books can add to the class resources

Sunset, still, over
shining sand.
The sad sea's
farewell to evening.

Conclusion

CAPTION, superbly effective in enhancing children's writing

The computer can offer an unprecedented stimulus to all forms of language acquisition across the primary curriculum. Children appear to have a natural affinity for computer interaction and the careful class teacher may use this to great advantage.

The programs discussed are by no means definitive, as the software and hardware situation is changing. However, as mentioned in the opening chapter, there is widespread agreement about the appropriate use of computers irrespective of the system used, and whatever changes lie in store it is likely that the basic philosophy will remain unchanged. In conclusion, the point made earlier can be restated. The introduction of a computer into the classroom will lead to children using language, whether or not the programs used are designed for this specific purpose. For the hesitant teacher the message is 'Give it a try'. It is unlikely that this will lead to anything but enthusiasm.

Programs Mentioned

AMX Pagemaker
Caption
Developing Tray
Fleet Street Editor
Folio
Front Page Extra
Infant Tray
Interword
Pendown
Podd
Prompt/Writer
Storyline
Story Starts
Typesetter!
Wordplay
Wordwise Plus
Writer

References

Beard, R. (1988) 'Foreword' to *Micro-scope Special: Writing*, Newman College/MAPE.

Bullock, Sir Alan (1975) *A Language for Life* (The Bullock Report), London, HMSO.

DES (1988) *English for Ages 5 to 11 (Proposals for the National Curriculum)*, London, HMSO.

Doherty, J. (1987) *Podd Pack 1*, North Eastern Education and Library Board, Educational Computer Unit, Northern Ireland.

Gregory, A., Lyons, H. and Redfern, A. (1988) *Writers' Workshop*, Monograph : University of Reading.

Gusdorf, G. (1975) *Speaking*, Evanston Ill., N.W. University Press.

Hammond, R. (1984) *The Writer and the Word Processor*, London, Coronet Books.

Hunter, P. (1988) 'The Writing Process and the Word Processor', in *Micro-Scope Special: Writing*, Newman College, MAPE.

Moy, R. (1986) *The Language Pack*, MEP.

Murray, D. (1988) 'Literature and the Micro in the Primary School, in *Micro-Scope*, 20, Newman College/MAPE.

Shenk, C. (1985) 'Good Practice', in *Times Educational Supplement*, 3583, March 1.

Wallen, M. (1988) 'A Rich Resource' in *About Writing (The National Writing Project Newsletter)*, London, SCDC.

5 Project Work: Religious Education

Monica Hughes

Various phrases have been used to describe a cross-curricular approach to learning in the primary school. These include topic or project work, Integrated Studies, Thematics, Humanities, Centres of Interest and Environmental Studies. The characteristics of project work have been described as follows:

1. Most topic work is in fact inter-disciplinary, not simply thematic.
2. Topic work involves active learning (visits, finding out from reference material etc.).
3. The learning is likely to be in pairs or groups rather than in individual or whole class contexts.
4. End-products in the form of presentations or displays may be typical of this approach.
5. The implicit role of the teacher is that of wise facilitator rather than instructor. (Kerry and Egglston, 1988).

It is essentially a way of working which involves

first hand experience
discovery methods
use and development of basic skills
without specific subject boundaries.

The amount of time any class may spend on their 'Project' might range from the majority of the week with the exception of fixed slots for basic subjects (although these may well be included) to perhaps only half a day a week.

Although the advantages of this way of working are well documented, there is sometimes a lack of planning for work of this type. The *First School Survey* (DES, 1982) found that only 30 per cent of the teachers planned their topic work and even this was usually on a termly basis. Even where planning does take place, flow charts and topic webs are often so diverse and wide-ranging that the curriculum becomes fragmented and there is little depth to any of the work because such a wide variety of activities are being undertaken. The ILEA *Junior School Project* (1985a) identified 'sessions of limited focus' as one of the characteristics of an effective school. This was linked to a 'work-centred environment' where not too many things are going on at any one time. Perhaps this could also be a suggestion for improving the quality of topic work in schools. If we are to limit the range of subjects involved in any topic we need to decide which will be studied together and which independently. *The Primary Survey* (DES, 1978) found that most topic work generally involved History, Geography and Science and sometimes Religious Education whereas *Improving Primary Schools* (ILEA, 1985b) showed that there was little emphasis on RE. In recent years there have been many exciting developments in the area of Religious Education and whilst the potential of the computer for supporting this particular area of the curriculum is perhaps not as obvious as for others, there are in fact a variety of ways in which RE can be enhanced with the help of the micro.

Religious Education in Topic Work

RE can be studied as part of a Humanities-based topic but it can also be developed as a distinctive area of study. Most topics in primary school will fall into three main categories in relation to RE:

(i) 'Topics in which no specific contribution to *explicit* R.E. objectives is envisaged ... however any topic which develops children's ability to reflect on experience has relevance to religious understanding' e.g. Animals, Transport

(ii) 'Topics in which R.E. is one of a number of disciplines employed to illuminate a topic' e.g. Buildings, Signs and Symbols, Communication

(iii) 'Topics in which R.E. objectives have a central place' e.g. Divali, Weddings, Pilgrimages (Hampshire, 1986).

It is important to emphasise that RE involves more than a *study* of the outward signs of religion. It is 'different from other subjects not just in content but in the emphasis it places on the *exploration* of the content as a means by which the subject's aims are realised' (Read, Rudge and Howard, 1986). Religion needs to be presented as a living and contemporary aspect of life and children helped to an awareness that matters of belief are often controversial and represent different outlooks and interpretations of experience. It involves an examination of the ways in which beliefs affect behaviour and are reflected in an individual's values and attitudes.

The aim of Religious Education is 'to contribute educationally to the development of pupils as individuals and members of society by fostering a reflective approach to life in the context of a growing understanding of the experience, beliefs and religious practices of mankind' (Bedfordshire, 1985).

The Adventure Game DRAGON WORLD

This is an excellent program to use for developing Religious Education as the *main* discipline employed to explore the topic of Treasures. The adventurer's task in Part 1 is to reach DRAGON WORLD having found the five magical teeth of Belogo *en route*. This involves lots of puzzles and riddles which will delight the children. They are also required to feed baby dragons and enlist the help of three sorcerers who behave like a fruit machine until they are chosen. The difficult final task involves following a route through a pitch dark cave, where friendly skeletons appear to warn you if you stray too far from the path. When all the five teeth have been found (and this will require more than one run through of the program) the password necessary to start Page 2 is revealed. The players' aim is now to find and collect five treasures which can be presented to the dragons and which they 'will be able to share forever'.

There are three main categories of treasure:

commodities	foods	'real treasure'
gold	worms	peace
emeralds	bananas	love
money	carrots	happiness
silver	cat food	laughter
rubies		kindness

Some of the items might not be regarded as treasures by the children and it is only as the game progresses that they learn the value of worms, for example. They are essential food for the badger and invaluable to the adventurer as they can be exchanged for another treasure. When five 'real' treasures have been collected and offered to the dragons the following message appears: 'Now the treasures have been found the world may be a happier place — but that will be another story'. The program

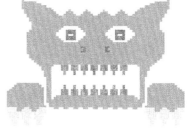

The not-so-scary dragon in DRAGON WORLD

is accompanied by extra supplementary software programs (DRAGON MUSIC, RIDDLE SOLVER, MAZES, THE RIDDLES) and three books which include a book of ideas for teachers and the Story of Dragon World. There are also a number of other items including an audio tape with the Story of Dragon World on one side and the original music on the other.

Three areas of focus for Religious Education in the primary school can be identified (Read, Rudge and Howard, 1986) and all of these can be developed from DRAGON WORLD.

1. Reflecting on human experience
   — by examining Concrete Treasures
2. Children's individual views and outlook
   — by examining Abstract Treasures
3. Religious beliefs and practices
   — by visiting Treasured Places
   — by discussing Treasured Books

Areas to Explore Before Playing DRAGON WORLD

The children can play the game with little or no introduction but their thinking will be developed (particularly in relation to Part 2) if some exploration of the term 'treasure' is undertaken. The younger the children, the more likely they are to think of treasures in concrete terms. They are unlikely to suggest such concepts as kindness, peace and happiness, which are introduced in DRAGON WORLD. This is not important at the initial stage as the primary emphasis at the start of the project will be on *Concrete Treasures*.

The main aims are to develop in the children an awareness that:

— different people value things differently
— precious things are too often taken for granted
— respect for people and their possessions is important (Merton, 1980).

Personal Treasures

Many children will respond enthusiastically to an invitation to bring into school something which they treasure, and it will not be difficult to amass a varied collection of objects. To help the child reflect on the idea of treasured possessions it will be necessary to try to classify the different kinds of items produced, perhaps by asking some of the following questions:

Is it a souvenir?
— where did it come from
— who chose it
— is it easily identified as coming from a particular place
— is its origin not immediately apparent
    — except to people who have been there or those who know its significance
— would everyone who went to the place choose the same souvenir
— how were souvenirs chosen

> I took in my autograph of Linford Christie because I saw him win the 100 metres. I waited a long time because there were lots of children waiting. I thought he would win a medal at the Olympics and he did. He is the best runner in England.
>
> Robert

Is it a reminder?
— of a place
— a time
— an experience
— a period of your life

Is it a favourite thing?
— why
— was it made, bought, given by someone special
— with what special occasions is it associated
— do other people have one just the same
— does no one have one just the same

Is it a mascot?
— for which group or individual
— does everyone recognize it as such — does it only have meaning to a special group
— how was it selected as a mascot
— why is it important

A treasured teddy

— does it help to identify the team, or perhaps bring good luck, offer consolation

Is it a trophy?
— was it a reward for achievement
— what was involved in the achievement
— do many other people have a similar trophy
— is it highly prized
— was it obtained with difficulty
— does its uniqueness contribute to its value

Is it rare or unused?
— is it special because few other people have one the same
— was it difficult to obtain

Is it common?
— is it a popular item
— does having one allow entry into a 'treasured group'

Is it fragile?
— does it need to be handled with care
— where is it stored
— how is it cleaned

Is it old?
— does its age contribute to its specialness
— is it as old as the child
— is it treasured for that reason

Is it a symbol?
— does it have special worth beyond its immediate appearance
— is it invested with special experiences

Other areas to explore include keepsakes, records, memorabilia, emblems, charms, talismans.

Some children may not be willing or able to bring their treasures to school. They may be too large, or too fragile or just *too treasured*. Not all children find it easy to share things which are important to them and the teacher will need to handle this dimension of the work with sensitivity.

Family Treasures

Moving outward from the child's personal treasure it would be interesting to identify other items which are treasured by their family and find out why. It is unlikely that collections will be so easy to assemble but it may be possible to explore the concept of an *heirloom* through one or two examples. The previous classifications may still be appropriate and it will be useful to compare how many qualities are attributable to any one item.

By examining family treasures it may be possible to develop some explicit Religious Education, particularly if you have children representing different faiths. Each religious group has its own treasures which represent various dimensions of the beliefs and practices of participants. Because of the range and diversity of religious artefacts the children are likely to gain greater insight into the idea of Religious Treasure if one type of item is examined. Treasured Books is an ideal starting point.

Although some families will have no books at all, many families will have ones which are treasured but which have no special religious significance: photograph albums, books from their parents' childhood, guidebooks which represent happy holiday times. Members of different religious groups will have their own special books which are 'treasures' to their family and community. The idea of something being a treasure because it is regarded as 'holy' by a group of believers will need to be discussed, and many of the qualities attributed to personal treasures will be appropriate here.

Treasured Books

Although the six major faiths (Christianity, Judaism, Sikhism, Islam, Hinduism, Buddhism) represented in Britain today all have their own scriptures, their place *within* the different faiths is not the same. It is important that children are made aware of this so that erroneous comparisons are not made.

The Bible

The Christian scriptures are usually given the title 'Holy Bible' which indicates how it is treasured by believers. It is sometimes called the 'word of God' but Jesus is usually thought of as 'The Living Word of God'. The Bible is made up of the Old Testament (the same as the Jewish Tenakh) and the twenty-seven books of the New Testament. The Apocrypha is also included in the Roman Catholic Bible.

Help the children to appreciate how treasured the Bible is to Christians by

— making a collection of different shapes, sizes and translations of the Bible
— noting the quality and variety of the paper used and the different types of binding and embossing
— finding out about early handwritten Bibles and those which have been beautifully illustrated
— discovering how a Bible is used in Christian worship
— investigating times and places when Bibles have been banned or particularly treasured
— enjoying some of its stories, poems and songs and perhaps noting how different versions use slightly different words and phrases.

The Qur'an

The Qur'an is treasured by Muslims because it is believed to be the actual words of God (Allah) revealed to the prophet Muhammad. The word Qur'an means 'recitation'. It is written in perfectly rhyming Arabic and translation is not encouraged because some of its meaning will be lost in the process. Great care is taken to keep every letter accurate in writing or printing. It provides the Muslim with a complete guide to life.

Help the children appreciate the importance attached to the Qur'an in Islam by

— finding out how it is looked after at home or in the mosque:
    kept on the highest shelf in the house with nothing above it;
    wrapped in silk to keep clean;
    placed on a wooden stand or stool to avoid over-handling;
    only read by someone who is thoroughly clean.
— identifying Qur'an schools in the neighbourhood, perhaps at a Mosque or Islamic Centre, where boys and girls go to learn Arabic in order to read the Qur'an
— identifying which verse of the Qur'an is whispered into the ear of a new-born baby
— collecting postcards and other examples of the beautiful calligraphy used in the Qur'an.

Guru Granth Sahib

To the Sikh, the Guru Granth Sahib or Adi Granth is more than a treasured book: it is believed to be the Living Word of God. It is actively regarded as the last Guru or spiritual teacher. It is composed of hymns and teachings but has no stories. It has a central place in Sikh worship at the Gurdwara but is not common in Sikh homes. It is usually about the size of a large pulpit Bible.

Help children to investigate

— how respect for the Guru Granth Sahib is expressed:
  kept in a special room;
  raised above the head when carried;
  placed on a raised throne or takht in the Gurdwara;
  covered by a canopy and with a chaun (tan of animal hairs) a symbol of authority waved over it
— the way in which the book is used in naming a child:
  it is opened when the mother presents the baby at the temple and the first letters of the first hymn on the page become the first letters of the baby's name
— find out some of the stories about the ten Sikh Gurus but avoid dramatization which involves a child playing the part of a guru as this could cause offence.

Areas to Explore Whilst Playing DRAGON WORLD

At this stage in the topic the main focus will be on the notion of *Abstract Treasures*. It is intended that the children will

— begin to find answers to the questions:
  what is a true treasure?
  what is of value?
— the answers will not be easy to come to and will *not* involve statements of fact, but rather involve phrases like
  I think ...
  I believe ...
— appreciate that treasures are not necessarily objects
— acknowledge that they themselves are 'treasures' in a variety of ways.

The children's answers will be influenced by their previous exploration of the theme *Concrete Treasures* and their experiences of collecting the different treasures in Part 2 of DRAGON WORLD. Encourage them to describe how they decided which treasures to collect and at what stage they realized that 'bananas, carrots and cat food' could be regarded as 'treasures'. They can also be helped to identify what use each animal made of the items. The children will need to try to decide which of the other items available will be the ones which 'the dragons most desire'. This will help them identify what is a 'true treasure' in the Town of Treasures.

Treasured Senses

The senses are sometime spoken of as 'the gift of ... sight, hearing, taste, smell, touch'. Encourage the children to explore aspects of themselves which they may tend to take for granted.
  It will be important to stress

— **that their senses enable the child to have 'treasured experiences'**
    —they can **see** beautiful things around them, enjoy a sunset, wonder at a new-born chick, marvel at the intricacies of a dew covered spiders web
    —they can **hear** the first note of song, the excitement of a fairground, the victory cheer as their team scores a goal
    —they can **taste** the first fruits of autumn, **smell** the cake baking ready for their birthday treat and **touch** a wide variety of wonderful things.
— **not everyone has full use of all their senses**
    —they need to be aware of what it would be like to be without their treasured senses and so begin to appreciate them more fully
    —they can empathize with those who suffer permanent loss of at least one of their senses
    —the visually impaired child and the one who is partially hearing may use their other senses in a variety of ways.

Treasured Abilities

Children can be helped to identify just what they can do now, that they couldn't

— a year ago
— before they started school
— when they were babies.

An exploration of their senses will have started them thinking along these lines. It may be possible for them to identify abilities or achievements of which they are proud. Perhaps these are the result of particular effort, practice or struggle. They can examine whether an accomplishment is more highly praised because of the effort involved in achieving it. Abilities can also offer children hopes, ambitions and dreams for the future which in themselves may be treasured.

Treasured Experiences

The priority here would be to get beyond the actual physical experience to the *feelings* involved which made the experience special. Help the children to identify where they have been or what they have done which involved, among others, feelings of

— joy
— pleasure
— wonder
— happiness
— delight
— contentment.

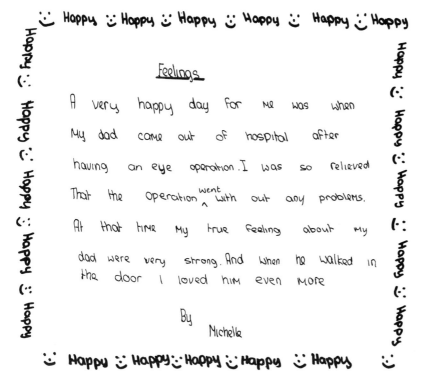

Happy ☺ Happy ☺ Happy ☺ Happy ☺ Happy ☺ Happy

Feelings

A very happy day for me was when My dad came out of hospital after having an eye operation. I was so relieved That the Operation went with out any problems. At that time My true feeling about my dad were very strong. And when he walked in the door I loved him even More

By
Michelle

☺ Happy ☺ Happy ☺ Happy ☺ Happy ☺ Happy ☺

It should also be stressed that treasured moments will not necessarily involve pleasure but might involve the opposite — for example, relief that something unpleasant has passed.

One day I went out. to feed my Rabbit
Called Sooky it was in the holidays
I found him lying in his hutch
We had him before I was born
I was very very sad we burwd
him in the rockery under flowers

When my cat ranaway I was heart broken, I cried
every night for hours, Three days later we had a
phone call from the local newsagents saying that
some one had seen the cat from the photo in the
window. So next day we went to the house
which my cat was in and I was overjoyed to see
him again

Treasured Qualities

These are perhaps the most abstract of all the treasures already explored. Start by identifying those on the program: friends, peace, kindness, health, warmth, laughter, love, happiness.

Help them explore what is actually involved in each. Are they mutually exclusive? If you possess one does it also involve others?

They might also identify others, for example, honesty, forgiveness, courage.

A synonym finder would be valuable here. Other words for honesty include fairness, truthfulness, openness, sincerity, frankness.

Areas to Explore After Playing DRAGON WORLD

When the game is completed and the 'true' treasures identified and collected, the children could begin the third stage of the topic by an exploration of the theme *Treasured Places*. This will combine the notion of both concrete and abstract treasures and draw together many of the ideas previously explored. It will also provide examples of how different people and places reflect such qualities as friendship, kindness, peace, etc. The work could involve implicit RE (with emphasis on the children's own Special Places), but more explicit work in RE could be undertaken through a study of Places of Worship in different religious traditions.

The main aims of this section would be

— to give the children factual knowledge of different types of religious buildings in their community
— to help them realize that particular religious buildings reflect the beliefs and practices of the community involved
— to help them imagine what it would be like to be a member of the community which particularly treasures a specific building and to appreciate more fully what the place means to believers.

This mosque is in Regents Park in London

Brendan

When visiting places of worship with children, some principles can be applied irrespective of which one is chosen.

1   Limit the amount of time to between half an hour and an hour so that the children have enough time to absorb some aspects of the place but are not overwhelmed by the experience.

2   The choice of which place to visit may be influenced more by the personality of the person who will show the children around and answer their questions than by the 'treasures' of the building itself.

3   Identify which particular treasures of the building, inside and outside, you intend to focus upon during the visit. Perhaps arrange the children into specific groups but don't overplan with worksheets and questionnaires. Remember that one of the aims of the visit is for the children to *experience* something of the meaning the building has for believers.

4   Prior to the visit find out which children already know the building well but don't expect them necessarily to be experts in their faith. Make a note of the children who have never been inside a religious building before — you may be surprised how many there are.

5   Encourage the children to be quiet when they first enter the building so that they can appreciate the atmosphere (you could link back to their earlier exploration of Treasured Experiences). Help them to identify what contributes to the special atmosphere:

— the lighting, its source and type
— the decorations, or lack of them
— the shape and size
— the smell
— the central or dominant feature
— the sounds, or lack of them.

6   Try to identify the different people who use the building and the variety of reasons for doing so. This will give the children further insight into why it is a Treasured Place for so many people but in a variety of different ways.

7   After any visit the children should be encouraged to write to thank the person who has shown them around, perhaps mentioning what memory of the visit they particularly treasured.

Treasures in Christian Places of Worship

There are likely to be many different types of building representing Christianity close to most schools, including churches (of various denominations and sects) and chapels. You may also be able to find a Cathedral, Minster, Abbey, Gospel Hall or a Salvation Army Citadel. Most will contain their own treasured items but the type and value attached to them will vary according to the beliefs of those involved.

Geographical Position
— is it on high ground and so visible from a wide distance?
— is it at the centre of the local community or perhaps at a crossroads of two major routes?

Architectural Features
— how does the design reflect the period in which it was built?
— how does the design reflect different beliefs within Christianity?
— how does the shape and size of one Christian building compare and contrast with others in the neighbourhood?

The Cross
— identify the different kinds found within the building
— note their position in relation to other objects
— what do the different types mean to Christians? compare a cross and a crucifix
— compare those on gravestones, hymn books, clothing, kneelers, memorials, cards
— make a collection of different types of crosses.

Robes and Vestments
— identify which Christian group use these
— find out their names
— what do different colours mean
— how are the different items put on
— what rituals are associated with the act of dressing
— find out who made the various items and how they are cared for.

Altar/Table
— find out how important this is in the community involved
— is it decorated by cloths? if so what kind are they?

— look at the places of various items on the altar
— find out the names and importance of them.

Vessels
— find out how the community celebrates Holy Communion; are bread or wafers used?
— what vessels are used?
— where are they stored, before and after the service?
– how are they used during the service?

Lectern
— note where the Bible is placed
— how is the stand decorated?
— what type of book is it — relate this to their earlier work.

Stained glass, pictures, statues and wall plaques can also be examined while on visits to some Christian buildings.

Treasures in Jewish Synagogues

The different traditions within Judaism (Orthodox, Reform, Liberal Progressive) are reflected in the types of synagogue to be found in Britain today.

The term 'synagogue' comes from the Greek, meaning 'gathering' or 'meeting place'. Traditionally, a synagogue has three functions for the community which are reflected in its different titles, the latter being the most popular:
Beth Tefillah — house of prayer
Beth Hamidrash — house of study
Beth Haknesset — house of assembly.

Architectural Features
— is it purpose-built or has it been adapted and modified for the community's use?
— how does it compare and contrast with other buildings in the environment?

The style of a synagogue tends to reflect the design of the time or place — so a European synagogue may look similar to a church whereas in the Middle East it may resemble a mosque.

Internal Layout
— is there a gallery or screened section?
— find out how it is used

— if not, what does this indicate about the position of men and
women during a service?

The Ark
— on which wall is the cupboard placed?
— find out why
— examine the different components
— find out their names and function.

Treasures within the Ark include:

The Parochet or curtain covering the Ark
— is it embroidered with any Hebrew words? if so find out
what they mean

The Mantles — or covers for the scrolls
— examine the messages embroidered on the velvet
— find out in whose memory they were given
— identify the different types of decoration used on the covers

Silver Decorations/Bells
— find out who presented the decorations to the community
and why
— investigate the function of the bells

The Yad
— note the way it is moved below a line of script to guide the
reader
— remember that Hebrew is read from right to left.

The Scrolls or Sifrei Torah
— where can the first five books of the Tenakh also be found?
— look at the way the scrolls are wound
— find out how the time of year is indicated by observing the
amount of parchment on each end of the scroll
— explore the festival of Simchat Torah when the reading of
the Torah is completed for one year.

Remember that the Sifrei Torah is a great treasure and is
always treated with respect.

Ner Tamid — Eternal Light
— what does the lamp indicate?
— of what is it a remembrance?
— if there is an inscription find out what it means.

The Menorah
— compare the seven-branched candelabra (an ancient symbol of the Jewish people) with the eight-branched candlestick used at the Festival of Chanukah
— why do you think the 'servant light' is so called?

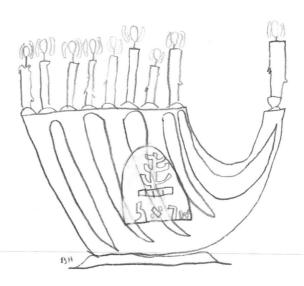

The Star of David, Prayer Shawl (tallit) and Skull Cap (yamulkah) could also be examined as treasured items within Judaism.

Treasures in the Hindu Mandir

Unlike Christian and Jewish places of worship, a Mandir or temple is not intended chiefly as a meeting place, although in Britain they are usually the centres where the Hindu community gather for a variety of reasons. The Mandir is designed primarily as a house for the spirit of God. It contains statues of god and goddesses which represent, for believers, the various facets of the one true god.

Architectural Features
— is it purpose-built or is it a converted church or large house?
— what evidence is there, from the outside, that it is a treasured place for Hindus?

The Shrine

— note first impressions, particularly the initial impact on the five senses

— find out who looks after the shrine and what is involved

— identify the different kinds of offering presented at the shrine and find out what happens to any food which is brought by worshippers

— identify the different images representing God — these may be in the form of statues, pictures or other symbols and may include some of the following:

Lord Rama — identified by his famous bow, will be familiar to many children as the central character in the story associated with Divali
Sita — wife and consort of Lord Rama renowned for her faithfulness

Hanuman — the monkey god who saved Sita from the evil Ravana
Lord Krishna — with his favourite flute, he inspires and gives love. His consort is *Radha*. Find out more about them through the festival of Holi.
Ganesha — the elephant-headed god who is regarded as the remover of obstacles. Find out how he came by his elephant head.

Many Hindu homes will also contain a shrine and worship will be conducted here on a daily basis.

The Canopy
— identify the way in which the shrine is covered
— is it an awning, pyramidical cover or symbolic representation?
— find out how this is used to show honour to the deity.

The Aarti — the offering of light
— identify the flat tray with its five wick holders or branches
— find out how the Aarti is presented at the shrine
— find out what is placed in the tray by each member of the congregation
— re-enact an individual receiving the Aarti:
    — after touching the sacred flame with both hands, the eyes are covered and the hands pass over the crown of the head and back to touch the heart.

The tilak or mark of worship
— find out how the red paste is made
— why is it placed in the figures and pictures on the shrine?
— compare the tilak — the red mark on the forehead given and received in worship as a mark of love and respect — and the tikka — a cosmetic red mark that women wear as a sign of marriage.

Other aspects to explore include the religious symbol of AUM, the distinction and offering of Prasad, and the use of music to accompany worship.

Conclusions

The suggestions in this chapter have focused upon both implicit and explicit Religious Education. The means by which the ideas are developed in the classroom will involve other areas of the curriculum, especially spoken and written language, the creative arts, including dance, drama and music and a variety of children's literature.

As the 'Treasure' topic draws to a close it is important to undertake an evaluation in order to identify which aspects were particularly successful and suggest areas where improvements could be made. The teacher should also address two specific questions in connection with this topic:

1. To what extent have the aims for Religious Education in general, and for each section in particular, been realized?
2. What has been the effect on the children's learning of a topic of 'limited focus'?

Programs Mentioned

Dragon Music
Dragon World
Mazes
Riddle Solver
The Riddles

References

Bedfordshire (1985) *Religious Education: A Planning Guide*, Ampthill, Teaching Media Resource Service.
DES (1978) *The Primary Survey*, London, HMSO.
DES (1982) *First School Survey*, London, HMSO.
Hampshire (1986) *Paths to Understanding: A Handbook to RE in Hampshire Schools*, McMillan.
ILEA (1985a) *The Junior School Project*, London, ILEA.
ILEA (1985b) *Improving Primary Schools*, London, ILEA.
Kerry, R. and Eggleston, J. (1988) *Topic Work in the Primary School*, London, Routledge.
Merton (1980) *Seeds of Life: Approaches to RE in the Primary School*, London Borough of Merton.
Read, G., Rudge, J. and Howard, R. (1986) *The Westhill Project RE 5–16: How do I teach RE*, Mary Glasgow.

6 Project Work: Adventure Games

Sue Underhay

The computer has many and varied applications in the primary curriculum, but possibly one of the most exciting is the use of Adventure Games. The name of this type of software could be misleading, since the programs are not in fact games at all, but new worlds for the child to encounter, experience and explore.

An Adventure program sets out to create a fantasy world in which the child has various adventures. A number of problems are posed and tasks set in order to complete the journey and, for its successful completion, a record of locations visited and decisions taken must be kept. This information is then used to help plan the strategies that will enable the successful completion of the mission.

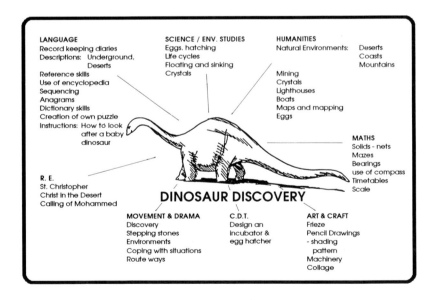

This type of software not only provides the environment for a great deal of group cooperation and social interaction among the children; it also acts as the focal point for the development of a wide variety of skills across the curriculum. The topic web centred around DINOSAUR DISCOVERY gives some indication of the possible skills and content areas this type of package can help to develop.

There are a number of different pieces of software for a variety of age groups which fit into the category of Adventure Games. 4Mation, a company based in Barnstaple, Devon, has developed a range of programs which have proved very popular and their titles include GRANNY'S GARDEN and DRAGON WORLD which are very suitable for young children, and DINOSAUR DISCOVERY and FLOWERS OF CRYSTAL for older children. This age range is only a guide as it is possible to use such programs across a wide age range. The more recent WORLD WITHOUT WORDS is a further example of an Adventure program with potential for use throughout the primary school. Simulations are very similar to Adventure Games, but are set in the real world rather than being based on fantasy, and these are discussed by Anthony Hunt in Chapter 7.

Classroom Organization

When using this type of software it is essential that it forms part of an integrated approach to classroom management, otherwise many of the values to be derived from its use will be lost. It is also important that the children are able to use the computer for an extended period of time, or at least have regular access for a couple of days each week. It is extremely difficult to organize both resources and children for this type of project if you can only have the computer for half a day at a time.

In my particular school use of the computer by a group of children fits in with all the other daily activities.

Each Monday morning children in my room are given a list of tasks and activities which they will be required to complete during the week. This we call 'Work for the Week'. Some of the activities will be of an individual nature, while others will require the children to work together in groups. Some they will be able to get on with straight away, as they are a continuation of previous work, while others will need more detailed explanation from me. The purpose of the list is to enable the children to see what will be expected of them in the week, and to plan the order in which they will complete their tasks. In my room I place a lot of emphasis on the child's responsibility for his or her own work. I have found that the computer fits well into this form of organization.

Our approach to curriculum planning is from a Project or Thematic basis. Having outlined the skills and attitudes that we wish to develop in the children we then look at the content areas that will best help us to achieve these aims. These then form the centre of the planning webs, to which we relate as many of the areas of the curriculum as it is practically possible to include. This could be carried to ridiculous extremes with areas of the curriculum being dragged into the theme on the most tenuous of links.

About 60 per cent of the school week is spent on activities related to the theme. This allows for the development of other basic Maths, language and motor skills to go on alongside. If these can be related to the theme they are, if not, they can continue in their own right, thereby ensuring the all-important balance in the curriculum.

We are not fortunate enough to have a computer for each classroom, and until very recently ten classes have had to share two work stations. There are now four computers in the school, which allows each class to work with one for at least a term at a time.

The Central Theme

In our year planning we try if possible to choose at least one theme which will provide the opportunity for the development of group interaction skills. Adventure Games provide the ideal vehicle for this, and on this particular occasion the upper school classes decided to use FLOWERS OF CRYSTAL as the starting point for a project for half a term.

FLOWERS OF CRYSTAL takes the children to the beautiful Planet Crystal, where, long ago, a wise old lady called Rumala foresaw dreadful things happening. As a safeguard against future disaster she hid five objects at various locations on the planet: a bag of soil, some special mineral fertilizer, an enchanted golden pot, and some magic spell-water, along with the last seed of the Crystal Flower. This she weaves around with various spells and enchantments, so that it may not be discovered by accident. As the years pass Rumala's fears are realized and the environment of the Planet Crystal is rapidly destroyed. The children are required to help find the hidden objects and in so doing help to save the Planet Crystal from destruction. On their journeys they will encounter a variety of problems and hindrances which they will need to outwit or

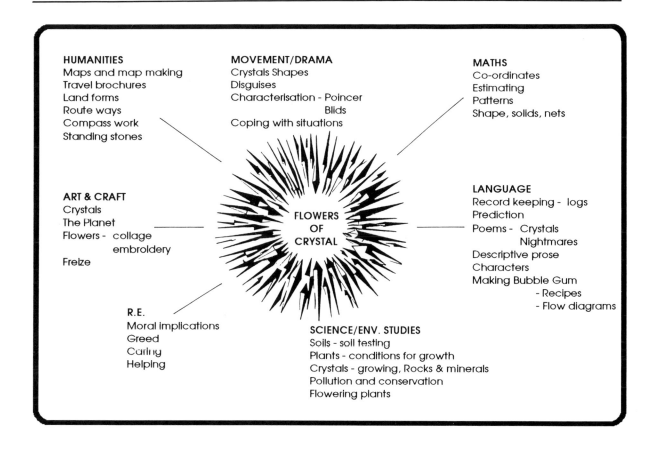

HUMANITIES
Maps and map making
Travel brochures
Land forms
Route ways
Compass work
Standing stones

MOVEMENT/DRAMA
Crystals Shapes
Disguises
Characterisation - Poincer
                     Blids
Coping with situations

MATHS
Co-ordinates
Estimating
Patterns
Shape, solids, nets

ART & CRAFT
Crystals
The Planet
Flowers - collage
            embroidery
Freize

LANGUAGE
Record keeping - logs
Prediction
Poems - Crystals
            Nightmares
Descriptive prose
Characters
Making Bubble Gum
            - Recipes
            - Flow diagrams

FLOWERS
OF
CRYSTAL

R.E.
Moral implications
Greed
Caring
Helping

SCIENCE/ENV. STUDIES
Soils - soil testing
Plants - conditions for growth
Crystals - growing, Rocks & minerals
Pollution and conservation
Flowering plants

overcome if they are to help the planet. The diagram above shows how this piece of software can form the core of a complete scheme of work right across the curriculum, and gives an indication of the types of skills and activities which can stem from it.

Case Study

The adventure program was used by a class of 9- to-11-year-olds, and was to form the centre of a six-week project.

A computer area was created in the corner of the classroom, in order to focus the groups' attention on the Planet Crystal. The display in this area contained predominantly art work relating to the project, together with copies of the story and supplies of the record sheets the children would need to keep an account of their experiences. A chart recording the groups' visits to the Planet Crystal was also displayed.

Grouping

The children worked in groups of three or four. A larger group would have found difficulty in sitting comfortably around the computer and having access to the keyboard. This size also allows for each child to have a specific job or role to perform: operating the keyboard, reading the screen display, or recording information and decisions taken.

Working in groups of three, each child can take a turn at each job

In the slightly larger group two children would work together on the latter task. The composition of the groups is also extremely important. The children need to be matched so that they will work together well and avoid any possible clashes. There are many different criteria for grouping children: age, sex, language ability, personality, friendship groups. Each teacher knows their class and I do not feel that there are any hard and fast rules; group composition depends upon the children one is working with at the time.

I prefer, wherever I can, to have mixed groups, although this is not always possible, and I tend to use personality and friendship groupings as my main considerations. I feel that these are important in order to avoid more dominant children taking over the group and always getting their own way. This, however, can also have its disadvantages, since a group of extroverted children can spend a lot of time putting across their own ideas about what the group should do, and not listening to the views of others. Teaching a vertically age-grouped class, I do not tend to group children according to age, as I feel general maturity and attitude to be of more importance. If there are any children with particular language difficulties, I will usually group these with children of a similar personality, or with a friend, on the understanding that they will help each other.

When using FLOWERS OF CRYSTAL with my class I divided the children into eight mixed groups, with personality and social patterns being my prime considerations. There were five groups of four and three of three. For most groups this composition worked extremely well, although it is interesting to note that the group who found greatest difficulty in working together, and who were one of the last to find the Crystal Flower, were four intelligent and very out-going individuals!

Introducing the Program

The program was introduced to the class as a whole towards the end of the second week in January. Initially the children listened to the tape recording of the story, all except the final paragraph. The story was faded out just before this point. There then followed a discussion of what the children thought the planet might be like in its early days, and how Jim would find it now. This acted as a stimulus for some art work. The children were asked to produce a picture, in pastels, of how they imagined the

Planet Crystal might have looked in Rumala's time. The children had already been introduced to the techniques necessary for using pastel, and this provided an ideal opportunity for them to put those skills into practice. It would also provide display material to help create the Crystal environment.

At the beginning of the following week the children listened to the story again, the complete version this time. The story was then discussed from the point of view of their task in helping Jim to save the planet. In order to save time, the children were shown the first few screen displays of the program and discussed the possible decisions they might make regarding equipment. We also took a look at the map of the planet. At this point the children were told of the groups they would be working in, and the routine that they would follow when visiting Crystal.

Classroom Organization

The children's first visit to Crystal was to be half an hour in length, and this enabled each group to see the planet on that first

Crystal collage

Most of the work takes place away from the computer

day. As the school day divided itself roughly into four one-hour sessions it was possible for a chart to be drawn up, taking account of such activities as PE, Games, Music and so on, showing which sessions the groups would be at the computer. This enabled the organization of the hardware to be carried out by the children themselves: by checking on the chart, they knew when they would be using the computer next. It enabled the groups to change over with the minimum of disruption, and also gave the children the independence of being able to plan when they were going to tackle some of their away-from-the-computer activities.

The groups were nominally allowed forty-five minutes for each visit, as this was felt to be a suitable amount of time for them to be in front of a computer screen. However, it also allowed for a certain measure of flexibility. If a group were nearing the end of their stay but felt they were within reach of something important then they had the time to continue, thereby avoiding the frustration of having to finish because it was lunch time or the end of the day.

This form of organization meant that each group spent up to two hours at the computer each week, in two sessions. It also allowed for an information-swapping session at the end of each week. I found these to be particularly interesting and useful sessions. My role was that of chair, ensuring that one group did not dominate the discussion. Each group was given an opportunity to talk about where they had been, what problems they

Grubble, the villian of the piece

had encountered, and to give tips to others without giving too much away. It also meant that normally quite reluctant children had the chance to make very positive contributions to a class discussion.

As the children began to use the program it became evident to many of them that they needed to keep very careful records of the places they had visited and the information they had gathered. They also soon realized the importance of planning, and using the information they had gathered on previous visits to avoid covering the same ground twice. Some groups, however, were going round in circles, collecting the same information without any clear idea of how to use it. The information swaps proved to be particularly useful for these children. Three of the eight groups needed extra help from me to begin to put the information they had gathered into some sort of order and to decide upon a plan for future visits.

Progression

By the end of the second week, four of the eight groups had found the treasures hidden by Rumala, and were ready to go onto the second part of the program. This made the Friday information swap particularly interesting, since those children had to decide how to share their findings without giving away any of the answers! It took up to another three visits for the remaining groups to find all four treasures. One group were particularly unlucky — the influence of the random element! While they knew exactly where to find each object, and had drawn up what appeared to be a logical route around the planet, something always went wrong! I could sympathize with them as, much to the children's amusement, I have still not completed the first part of the program without being Pounced or Fright Frieked! As the children were determined that they wanted to finish the first part (if only to beat the system!) I spent two extra lunch-time sessions working with them to enable them to have completed a successful mission by the end of the third week. Full credit to those four children for perseverance!

Meanwhile half of the class had started on the second part, the quest for the last Flower of Crystal. Here they were presented with a different set of problems, and different groups experienced different difficulties.

Children who had appeared to sail through the first part were now beginning to struggle a little, while others who had had a

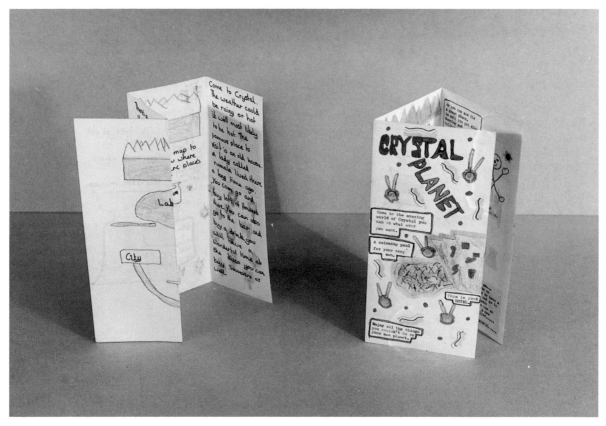

Travel brochures for Crystal

problem getting started were now coming to terms with the tasks. It took three more weeks for all of the groups to find all of the flower parts.

After each visit to the Planet Crystal the children were required to keep an individual log of what had happened to them, the decisions they had taken and the reasons behind their decisions. At various times they were also encouraged to include detailed descriptions of the characters they had met, and maps, diagrams and illustrations of the places they had visited. These activities formed a major part of the children's general language work for the duration of the program. To begin with, log entries from some individuals were a little sparse, but as the weeks passed these became more and more detailed. This was particularly rewarding for those children who had previously struggled to express themselves on paper.

*Crystal designs using DELTA
(see Chapter 9)*

Associated Activities

At the school in which I work a strong emphasis is placed upon presentation and so the children were also encouraged to decorate their work in an appropriate way. This was finally bound into a booklet for them to take home at the end of the term.

Alongside the computer work, many other 'Crystal-related' activities were taking place, some individually as part of the child's 'Work for the Week', and others as group tasks. The activities that I chose to follow with my children came about largely as a result of their interests. However, I always kept my objectives in mind, in order to ensure a match between what I wanted the children to achieve and their interests.

Each child produced a small travel brochure, expounding the attractions of Crystal.

We investigated crystals in great detail, making 3D models of solids, creating collages, collecting various mineral crystals and investigating these under a microscope where possible. We grew crystals, and some children created their own designs for Crystal Flowers using DELTA (see Chapter 9), while others used triangular grid paper for their designs.

In groups the children looked at other plants with unusual characteristics, and some produced detailed drawings of flowering plants.

Many children showed an interest in the illustrations in the accompanying booklets, and attempted to create their own illustrations for the story using similar techniques.

In Music the children created their own sound effects to accompany the appearance of the Blids, Pouncer, or the Fright Friek; and in Movement and Drama we attempted to develop and portray the Blids, Pouncer, Rumala and Grubble. In Creative Language work we looked at dreams and nightmares, and the children wrote about their dreams and created nightmare poems. Much of this work was put together in a classroom display for other children to visit before the half-term break. Some of it was also used as a basis for a class assembly, shown to the rest of the school on the Friday after half-term.

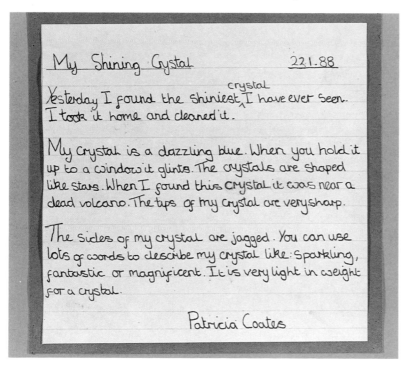

My Shining Crystal   221.88

Yesterday I found the shiniest crystal I have ever seen.
I took it home and cleaned it.

My crystal is a dazzling blue. When you hold it
up to a window it glints. The crystals are shaped
like stars. When I found this crystal it was near a
dead volcano. The tips of my crystal are very sharp.

The sides of my crystal are jagged. You can use
lots of words to describe my crystal like: sparkling,
fantastic or magnificent. It is very light in weight
for a crystal.

Patricia Coates

Almost all of the children expressed some concern about the affect that Grubble's antics were having on the planet, which in turn led to a discussion of what we were doing to our own planet. This turned our attention towards pollution and the need for conservation of special areas. I had initially intended that the work arising from Flowers of Crystal would last for the first half of the Spring term, approximately six weeks; however, the children's interest was so aroused that I decided to continue with the theme after the half-term break, and Pollution and Conservation became our area of study for the rest of the term.

Part of the final display

This enabled me to further develop their research, planning and presentation skills, group cooperation (they continued to work in their crystal groups, with minor modifications), and their environmental awareness. This project in its turn also led to an end-of-term display.

I was extremely pleased by the way this project captured the children's enthusiasm and carried us all along paths I had not intended to tread. The standard of the work produced by most of the children was high, while some of those who had in the past struggled gained a wonderful sense of achievement. I also felt that it had been highly successful in a number of less measurable areas. It enabled me to see how different children go about gathering information and the strategies they devise for using this to solve the problems confronting them; it gave me an insight into how many of them think. It seemed to give many children the confidence to explain their ideas to an audience, and they became much clearer and more concise in their explanations, and certainly gained a great deal of enjoyment from their experiences on Crystal.

Programs Mentioned

Granny's Garden
Delta
Dragon World
Dinosaur Discovery
Flowers of Crystal
World Without Words

7 Project Work: Simulations

Anthony Hunt

As recently as 1978, when a major survey of primary education was made (DES, 1978), the role of the microcomputer in the primary curriculum was non-existent. Indeed, much criticism in that survey was of the lack of skills given in certain areas of the curriculum to primary children; also the impact of a group-orientated approach to education was minimal. Yet within five years, David Walton was writing in *Changing Schools...Changing Curriculum* (1983) of the invaluable introduction of the micro-computer into primary schools.

> It is hard to define this effect: it revolves around the non-threatening and relatively predictable nature of microcomputers that allows children to investigate and learn from their mistakes; it seems able to help with the development of skills of precision, logic and planning — more valuable and fundamental skills than the curriculum topic itself, which becomes a vehicle for this development.

This is exactly what the 1978 survey had suggested was lacking in the primary curriculum. Now, six years further on, our understanding of the practical versatility of the microcomputer has grown considerably and, with it, the part played by Simulation programs in the primary curriculum. Many schools have devised programmes of topic work or developing themes which form the spine of their curriculum. Of all computer applications, Simulation and Adventure programs equate most naturally with this vital process involving children's learning: cross-curricular education at its most effective.

At this point, a distinction should be drawn between the Simulation and the Adventure program. The former is based upon reality and the latter on fantasy, but much of what is mentioned here for Simulation can also be applied to Adventure. In effect, a Simulation is based around a set of real circumstances into which the children can enter, experimenting and experiencing, without having the ability to alter the original facts or circumstances. It would be nonsensical for children, using the program 1665, to be able to solve the problems of the Plague of London: instead, they should experience the frustrations and the mounting panic of a committee trying to make moral and social judgements when events are almost beyond their control.

Whether the Simulation theme is historical, geographical, scientific, social or environmental, programs are available which can enhance that theme, providing either an added dimension or, in the case of some of the major packages mentioned later, forming the central core of the topic.

A recent document circulated to all primary schools in Hampshire, *Computers in the Primary Curriculum* (1988), includes a section on the power and importance of Simulation and Adventure material in the present-day primary curriculum:

> The strategies that children develop will prove of great value as they grow, learn and mature: having to listen to someone else's point of view; learning to cooperate with others: coping with the need to discuss coherently the pros and cons of a certain course of action: developing tolerance, perseverance and vision; having to learn from their mistakes and accepting the consequences; gaining self-confidence and developing logical thought.

The children's enthusiasm for Simulation programs (which have been properly researched by teachers and which are relevant to the children and the curriculum) extends far beyond the two-dimensional computer screen. Only a small percentage of the day is spent at the keyboard; the rest of the time is involved with artistic, creative, linguistic and investigative work synonymous with the thematic approach. Visits to places involved in the program (e.g. Southsea Castle for MARY ROSE or the British Museum for EXPEDITION TO SAQQARA) help enrich the children's understanding and make the simulated first-hand experience real. Word-processing and database programs can be used to support the extension work. Electronic mail can also provide an added impetus on occasions, and programs like NEWSROOM EXTRA can create valid simulation experience for children of all ages. As with all good primary practice, the successful use of a Simulation program depends upon the organization which precedes it.

Organization

'We did Flowers of Crystal last week and want something different for this week.' It is surprising how many teachers still regard Simulation and Adventure programs as something out-side their normal curriculum work — a sort of in-filling strategy for those children who finish their 'real work'. Of course, it is possible to use the programs in isolation, particularly when computer resources within an individual school are limited. Although the ideal mentioned in the previous chapter of having the computer system full-time for a half-term period is not always possible or practical, a term's Simulation topic can be organized on one-day-a-week access with all of the extension work being carried out during the remaining four days. Two days a week would be better of course, particularly if other associated computer programs were required as mentioned above. However, the sooner every class base has direct access to a system all of the time, the sooner the computer will enhance our existing primary curriculum even more and then extend it into new and exciting areas.

There are two kinds of Simulation program: minor ones which can support an existing topic and major ones which become the central topic. In either case, the teacher will need to be familiar with both the program itself and the associated material which is provided or which will need to be researched separately. Once that has been done, the way in which the project is to be approached will differ from teacher to teacher depending upon the age of the children and the environment of the school. One development that the use of Simulation programs has encouraged is a more integrated approach to classroom organization. Only one group of children can work at the computer at any given time; the rest will be involved in various associated activities, either within their groups or as individuals. Consequently, decisions will need to be made about the composition of groups in which children work.

Experience has shown that, for Simulation and Adventure programs, groups of three or five children work more satisfactorily together. Many such programs contain stages when direct alternatives face the group (usually answered by Yes or No). A group of four children can reach a genuine stalemate, no matter how long they debate the pros and cons. However, even when four children out of a group of five opt for a particular course of action, the views of the fifth need to be discussed, for he or she may prove to be correct. Again, research shows that mixed-ability groups are generally preferable, particularly with younger children where at least one good reader per group is essential. Also a reasonable distribution of the sexes is necessary. Pauline Bleach's pilot study, *The Potential of Computers to Aid Understanding* (1986), stated:

> In all groups there was initial antagonism at having to cooperate with the opposite sex but in this progress was gradually made. In the few groups where one sex predominated, problems persisted longer, often with the isolated child being pushed away from the main focus of the group work.

The class teacher knows his or her children better than anyone, of course, and the match of personalities and abilities within each group is a matter for experience to determine. The academic children will give a lead in one direction, the artistic children in another, the creative children in another and so on, and those children whose social skills enable them to bring coherence and a sense of purpose to a group are particularly valuable. As one child said of the benefits of working in a group, 'All your brains think together'.

The siting of the computer system will depend largely upon the physical limitations of the school building. In many schools, the classroom itself is the only available place for the system. In other schools, it may be possible to position the computer between two classrooms, thus creating a greater flexibility of use, or even in a central area leading off to three or four class bases. Younger children do require constant assistance when working in groups. Unless parents can help in this way (given proper tuition in how to encourage groups without interfering or 'giving the answers' when the children are uncertain), the classroom will still be the most obvious place for the system, whatever the layout of the school. Older children work better away from the main class base where their (often noisy!) discussions cannot upset other groups who may be working in a quieter or more concentrated manner. The computer as a central resource also creates interest in children from other classes and helps generate a more exciting atmosphere. Should space permit, one excellent alternative is to 'build' the computer into a realistic environment such as a diving boat for MARY ROSE or

The 'police station control room'
quite naturally has computers. One
computer is being used to generate
in-coming calls, the other to
organize a response

a wigwam for WAGONS WEST! A number of schools, when using POLICE — LANGUAGE IN EVIDENCE, have set up a police control room which quite naturally includes a computer. The program generates incidents to which patrol cars have to respond, and includes a whole range of logistic problems: cars in for repair, hold ups caused by road works and so on. The children pictured in the photograph below were involved in a whole range of activities. In addition to the obvious potential for using language in various modes, the project involved rostering, devising recipes and cooking (for the police canteen), map work, coordinates etc. However this approach is not essential for if the program is good, the children will imagine themselves in the simulated environment whatever their surroundings.

Simulation programs provide cross-curricular experiences almost without exception, no matter what the central 'subject' area, and further examples of the cross-curricular work involved in five programs are included in the rest of this chapter. Teachers must be prepared to abandon to some extent their 'normal' curriculum if they are to get the best work out of a major Simulation. This course of action does mean that the teacher has to record accurately the various skills and experiences involved in the project, and from past experiences, parents are very receptive to the enthusiasm for work generated in their children.

Carrying out a Simulation topic with a class is not an easy option. It requires good organization and commitment from

The 'control room' has a visitor,
a police woman from the local
constabulary

the teacher, enthusiasm and involvement from the children, patience and tolerance from colleagues and an abundance of energy from anyone closely associated with it. The rewards are great and well worth the effort.

Software

The following five examples of major Simulation programs are simply that and represent only a small proportion of the programs available for your choice. All have been used in a cross-curricular way with upper junior classes and, although a few examples of the children's work and relevant photographs have been included, there is no substitute for the experience of seeing groups of children working together on such themes and topics.

EXPEDITION TO SAQQARA

EXPEDITION TO SAQQARA is a Simulation program based on the real archaeological site at Saqqara, one of the most

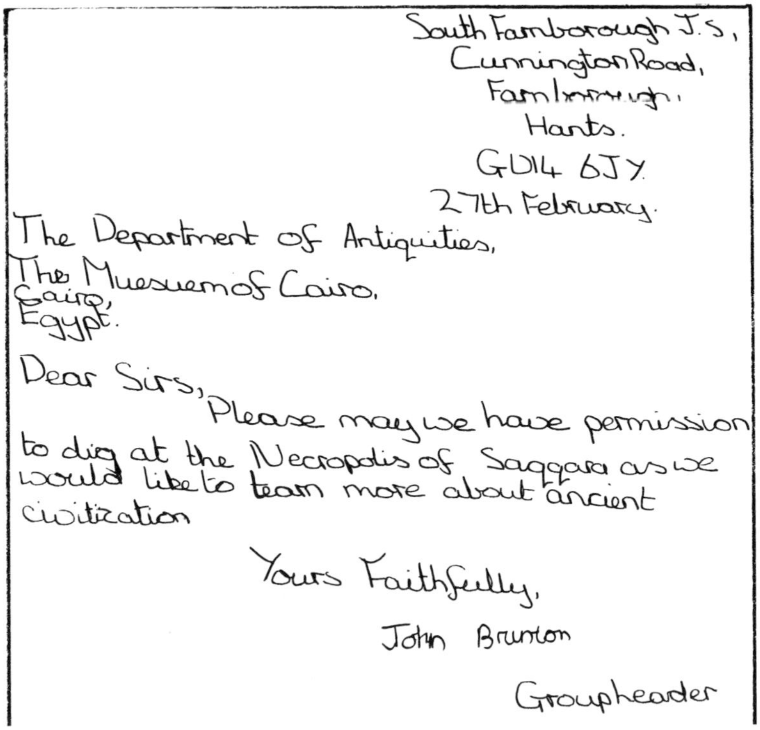

South Farnborough J.S,
Cunnington Road,
Farnborough,
Hants.
GU14 6JY
27th February.

The Department of Antiquities,
The Muesuem of Cairo,
Cairo,
Egypt.

Dear Sirs,
Please may we have permission to dig at the Necropolis of Saqqara as we would like to learn more about ancient civilization

Yours Faithfully,
John Brunton
Groupleader

```
                                              The Department of Antiquities,
                                               The Museum of Cairo,
                                                 Cairo,
                                                   Egypt.

       Our Ref. A.K./H.S.                         28  2 .84
       Your Ref. J.8/333

       Dear John Brunton

            I am pleased to issue you with permission to explore the necropolis
       of Saqqara.   Naturally, any finds are the property of the Egyptian
       government and permission must be obtained in order to remove items from
       the site.

            I wish you good fortune in your quest.

                       Yours sincerely,

                       AEKholy

                       Aly el Kholy
                       Director of Excavations
                       Department of Antiquities.
```

important in Egypt. It simulates the search for and excavation of ancient tombs and requires the children to mount a realistic expedition — to obtain grants and permission to excavate, to manage finances and teams of workers, to map out the site, to direct and record details of excavations and to research and speculate on the meanings of 'finds'.

Once permission has been granted by the Department of Antiquities in Cairo for excavation of the area and funding has been obtained from London University's Faculty of Archaeology, each group is free to search the desert for signs of a tomb before claiming it for their own and then carrying out a proper excavation. As there were fifteen groups of five children drawn from two vertically-grouped third and fourth year junior classes, and there are only sixteen tombs containing finds, it was decided to segregate the groups into four specific areas so that, eventually, each group could find and excavate a tomb of its own. Diaries were kept every time a new day's search was made and, by the end of the first week, all of the groups had found a tomb successfully.

The excavation of each tomb covers a 10 by 10 grid 6 layers deep (i.e. 600 coordinate points) with varying strata to be cleared: the harder the rock, the more hours required to clear the way and the less time before the funds run out. On the second occasion that the program was run, electronic mail was used to claim funds, with a neighbouring school acting as the Department of Antiquities in Cairo. As the children had communicated with France and Sweden, they did not question the using of electronic mail for Egypt. How small the world has become.

A 'find' is shown by a code and when the children told their teacher what the code was, the appropriate card showing the find was revealed for the first time. Each group became responsible for its own book: art work proliferated and the area was taken over with Egyptian drawings and artefacts; stories were written, an assembly was acted out, the British Museum was visited and so on. At the end of seven hectic weeks, there was still work left to do, the local travel agents had run out of brochures on Egypt (and wondered why no one actually booked any holidays there!) and an experience had been enjoyed by staff and children alike which will remain in the memory long after more mundane curriculum work has been forgotten.

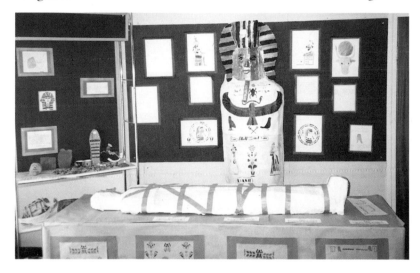

Part of the display following the 'Expedition to SAQQARA'

SUBURBAN FOX

SUBURBAN FOX is an environmental program in which children play the part of a fox trying to survive in an urban area. As the accompanying booklet states:

> In putting the children into this role-playing situation, the intention is to give them first-hand experience of the problems and hazards that a fox might encounter and

therefore to develop an empathy and emotional involvement that give their task a distinct purpose. The simple
objective is to use one's wits to survive for as long as
possible.

The program comes complete with two reference books,
activity cards and a large poster; the suggestions for support
material and project plans are good. This Simulation is best
suited for use in the winter term.

A fox-like environment was set up around the computer in an
area outside the class base. As with Saqqara, groups were
decided (the starting point for each group is set at random) and
the adventure was on to survive longer than any other group:
at the end of three weeks' strategy and planning, the most
successful group managed to stay alive for thirteen days
(although ninety-nine days' survival is one aim of the program!). Gradually the groups began to rationalize their movements, stopping as daytime approached rather than run
unnecessary risks. Each child kept his or her own diary (a sort of
Filofox!) and the problems encountered, which often ended in
the 'death' of the group as a fox, served as a constant reminder
of their dangerous life. The problem-solving nature of this
particular program created even more discussion and argument
than usual, not least when some actions led to the demise of the
unfortunate fox. As one group said: 'We tried out lots of ideas
so we got killed more often, but we found out more than the
other groups.'

In addition to the art and craft work which came from this
topic, the mathematical work on tracks, food chains, speed of
movement, etc., involved a variety of graphical work. As with
all such programs, the language at the computer exceeded in
richness and passion the written language which followed. The
whole school (not to mention the County Museum Service)
became involved in the teacher's frenetic search for a stuffed fox
to accompany the topic, all to no avail: the children had to wait
for a visit to Selborne before seeing one and then realized that
the fox was smaller than they had imagined. One boy saw a fox
in his garden which brought a first-hand reality to the topic. By
the end of the half-term's work, all of the children had come to
understand the plight of foxes driven into man's territory in an
effort to survive. The work stimulated by this program
exceeded expectations: at first, the theme seemed to be less
conducive to extensive development compared, for example,
with SAQQARA. However, the 'emotional involvement' of

the children created its own momentum and, unlike historical simulations where the opportunity to enjoy local experiences is limited by the subject matter to some degree, this simulation provided 'immediate' possibilities for the children as foxes were seen frequently in the urban environment surrounding the school.

WAGONS WEST

WAGONS WEST is one of four excellent Simulation packages from the same software house noted for its depth of detail in the associated Teacher and Pupil Guides: the pack comprises two discs, nine information sheets, eight group cards, two colour posters, 'Fitting Out' record sheets and an extensive Teachers' Guide. The theme of the Simulation is to follow the trail of the pioneers traversing America in the mid-nineteenth century, assuming the roles of 'real' people in the process.

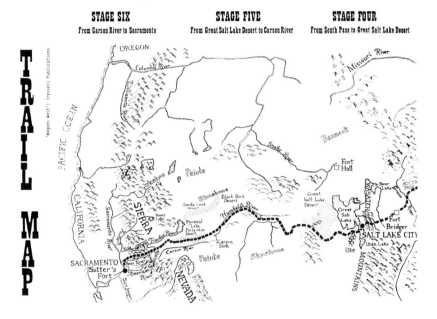

The pupils are transported back to another time and place — North America — 1852 — a high point in the opening up of the American far west. Taking the role of men and women in a group of emigrants, the pupils will make the longest, most exciting — and possibly most dangerous — journey of a lifetime. Travelling from their old homes in the Middle and Eastern states of North America (and often originally from Europe) they will

Planning the route to the west

This beautiful shirt was thought to have magic powers to protect the wearer from the white peoples bullets.

first gather and 'fit out' in one of the Missouri 'jumping off' towns, in this case Independence. They will then set off, as part of a wagon train, on a journey of over 2000 miles across grassy plains, high mountains and hot deserts, to reach a 'paradise on earth' — the promised land of California. On their long journey they will meet shrewd shopkeepers, rough and ready Mountain Men, have dealings with Indians, visit forts and encounter buffalo and other wild animals of the plains, mountains and deserts. (Teachers' Guide)

If ever the description of a program invited participation, this must be it. The program lived up to expectations.

Although the main theme of this Simulation is historical, other curriculum areas involved include geography, maths, drama (the whooping of wild Indians still echoes in my ears to this day!), art and craft, social and moral education (do you take the woman suffering with cholera or abandon her to her fate!), language, science, problem solving, music, book-making, drafting and redrafting, health education and so on. Consequently, this is a Simulation where the program forms the central topic and all areas of the curriculum evolve: if all of the associated work is followed through, there is little time for anything else! Unlike SAQQARA, but like the more recent 1665, WAGONS WEST actually involves the children in the experience by getting them to assume the character of a real-life pioneer (or Plague Committee member). Whilst they are at the computer, they cease to be themselves and take on the personality of relevant individuals. This can create emotive conflicts but also fascinating entries in the group's daily diary:

'2nd September. 1 woman died because of lack of water so we had to drive our wagons over her grave so that the Indians would not dig her up.'

'4th September. Tempers fled [flared] and a murder was commited so we sent him into the wilderness. We found his body. He had been killed.'

'24th September. 2 children went missing today. We decided to go on and leave them. We never saw them again, also no time could be wasted.'

'15 May. Today a woman came up to us and asked us to take her with us to California but we didn't because we didn't have enough food.'

'20 May. We found her body today. (The doctor on our wagon said she had been killed by CHOLERA). We were very, very lucky, our friend Marjarie was very shocked but didn't faint.'

Marjarie had given birth to a baby on April 30th and had previously fainted on May 11th after some trouble 'but some water soon woke her up.'

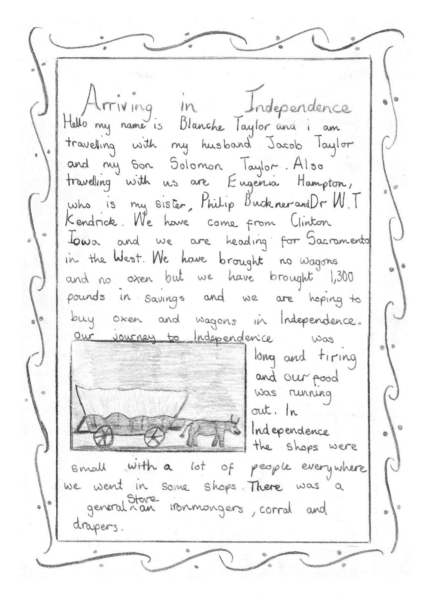

Arriving in Independence

Hello my name is Blanche Taylor and i am travelling with my husband Jacob Taylor and my son Solomon Taylor. Also travelling with us are Eugenia Hampton, who is my sister, Philip Buckner and Dr W.T Kendrick. We have come from Clinton Iowa and we are heading for Sacramento in the West. We have brought no wagons and no oxen but we have brought 1,300 pounds in savings and we are hoping to buy oxen and wagons in Independence. Our journey to Independence was long and tiring and our food was running out. In Independence the shops were small with a lot of people everywhere we went in some shops. There was a general store an ironmongers, corral and drapers.

These, and many other examples, illustrate vividly the personal involvement of the children in this project. The language used, both written and oral, was positive and exciting (as well as excited at times) and, as a consequence, the cross-curricular work which developed from the time spent at the computer (an average of twenty minutes a day per group) was of a very high standard indeed.

CARS — MATHS IN MOTION

CARS — MATHS IN MOTION is advertised as suitable for 8-year-olds to adults and was Educational Computing's top program of 1985 when it first arrived in primary (and secondary) schools. The aim of the program is for a group of children

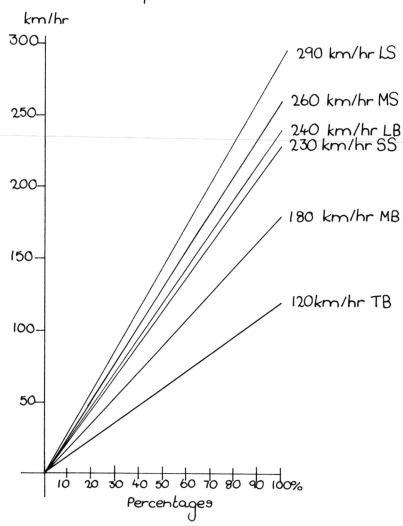

Calculating safe speeds, from tight bend to long straight

to set up a Grand Prix racing car and race it against other groups' cars on a specially prepared racetrack.

Each group has to take account of the weather, the precise speed of their car on every element of the track, engine tuning, aerodynamic downforces, suspension adjustments and gear-box ratios. Then, during a series of practice laps, they have to amend their numeric entries not only to get around one lap safely but also to do so as quickly as possible.

'Practice Lap Two. We lowered the speed on feature 19 down to 155 km/hr — we did exactly the same. We spun and crashed on feature 19. We reckon we must have measured the degrees on feature 19 wrongly so we will measure the degrees on feature 19 again then maybe we will be able to get round the track.' 'Practice Lap Three. We got a protractor and measured feature 19 again. And we found it was a tight bend not a medium bend and the safe speed for a tight bend was 120 km and our speed was 160 km. So we slowed it down to 102 km and that got us round the track in a time of 117.6.'

After Practice Lap Four their speed was down to 116.2; after Five down even further to 112.7; they were ready for the Great Race!

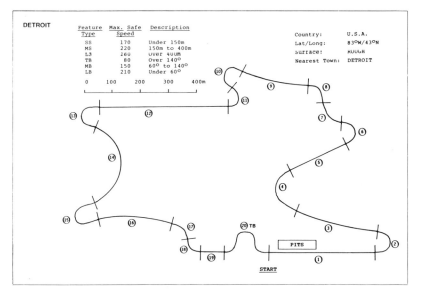

Each circuit involves different calculations of distance, angle and safe speed

'At the start of the race our car was in pole position. On the first four laps we stayed in 1st position then we were over taken by Stuart New on lap five. On the eighth lap we had a pit stop we changed our tyres to intermediate dry and we added 180 litres of fuel. Up to the 16th lap we were in 2nd position then we dropped down to 3rd place because we had a pit stop. We put 180 litres of fuel and changed our tyres to dry. Then on lap 20 we overtook David Thomas to regain second position we stayed second position until lap 30 when we overtook Stuart New and we won the race.'

SPORT REPORT

30p

13TH APRIL

WELL DONE 777 & 333

ZANDVOORT RACES

At the recent Grand Prix at Zandvoort Speed Steve won with a lead of 3 minutes from the second team 444. Well done 444 at least they survived the race! All the other teams went out of the race for various reasons. At the Zandvoort Grand Prix on the 12th of April Speed Steve soon gained the lead. Stephens team were precise about their fuel consumption. But they overlooked one little problem. They had to get to cross the finish line! Because Speed Steve was running low on fuel they let team 444 over take him. Team 777 won the race.

Speed Steve would have completed the race if he didn't run out of fuel on the last lap. 777 went through their race without a single fault. Well done 777. Next week we will be reporting on the Wimbledon Short Tennis Championship.

COOL HANNAH'S ICE CREAMS ONLY 2.00

A page produced using FRONT PAGE EXTRA (see Chapter 4)

For those of us used to the thrills of driving, the opportunity to share such an obviously exciting and problematical journey with a group of children in an educational environment is exhilarating — like the real thing!

As the title suggests the main thrust (no pun intended) of the program is mathematical despite all the language, science and art work which develops naturally along the way. Multiplication, division, geometry, graphs, scales, percentages, strategy: all of these are involved and more, but all of it in a context in which the children can see some purpose to the work expected of them. How different this is from the concept of mathematics as pages of sterile sums and meaningless problems presented in the rigid straitjacket of the maths lesson.

Just as SUBURBAN FOX represents a new approach to environmental work, so CARS achieves the same for mathematics. The development of similar programs in the future will create the climate within these two areas of the curriculum which exists already in the humanities, namely the cross-curricular emancipation of the primary curriculum.

The team log

```
*****************************************************
* First of all we did our workshop         *
* adjustments. We tuned Engine Tuning       *
* at 8 Aerodynamic, downforce at 7.         *
* Suspension adjustment at 8 and Gear       *
* Box Ratios at 8. These are the            *
* percentages we got. Short Straight        *
* 93%, Medium Straight 84% Long St. 79%*
* Tight Bend 81%, Medium Bend 88% and       *
* Long Bend 90%. Then after that we         *
* our safety checks. These are the          *
* safety checks we put in. Fire             *
* extinguisher, brakes, oil, engine         *
* coolant, fuel tank, seat belt, tyres *
* mirrors and instruments. Then we          *
* were allowed on the track. We got all*
* the way round number 12, and we had       *
* an engine blow out.                       *
*****************************************************
```

'They sure start diving early in England!'

MARY ROSE

MARY ROSE was one of the first genuine Simulation programs to be used in Primary schools, coinciding with the spread of BBC machines. The original version (which is still available) was textual only, allowing groups of children to find the site of the wreck and then dive, clear the mud and discover artefacts in the exact position where they were found originally. The latter was a complex process as the whole of the wreck was available to each group and the record-keeping necessary for a successful search proved too much for some groups, as did the frustration of failing to find anything. Nonetheless, the Simulation proved popular, particularly for those schools within reach of Southsea and the Mary Rose itself. On one visit, watched by an open-mouthed group of American visitors, two children found the real artefact that they had 'discovered' during the Simulation. 'There it is — that's what we found!' As one American was overhead to say — 'They sure start diving early in England!'

Recently, a more graphical version of MARY ROSE has been released. The principle is the same (except that the harbour search is no longer a part of the program) but the children watch the diver from vertical and horizontal positions as he clears the mud. Timbers can be seen as they are revealed and artefacts are marked. At any stage, a printout of the exact position of the wreck complete with a list of the artefacts found is available. This pack comes complete with photographs, posters and other information for the children to read. All of the usual work associated with such a theme is in evidence and, in the class base in which this project took place, when one group had finished diving (due to the lack of air) the next simply took over from the same position, which would occur in reality.

The Challenge

Much more could be said about the use of Simulation programs in the Primary Curriculum: only the briefest of introductions can be given here. The recently published Kingman Report (DES, 1988) has this aim as one of its targets for 11-year-olds (with a simpler version for 7-year-olds):

> Talk and listen, both in groups and in a whole class, in a variety of forms: narrating, explaining, justifying, describing situations and feelings, giving instructions and

conveying information, playing a role, putting forward and countering an argument.

What a shame that the members of that committee did not extol the virtues of the computer (through Simulation and Adventure programs particularly) as the perfect resource to enable the above target to become part of the educational process of every class in every school in all environments.

If you have never made use of Simulation or Adventure programs in your class base, now may be the time to start — you will not regret the decision and your children will enter worlds of experience with enthusiasm and a quest for knowledge and adventure not possible before. But remember, if you do take up the challenge, you will be embarking upon an educational adventure of your own in which you and your children can explore, learn, discuss, make decisions, solve problems and, above all else, learn to grow together. Bon voyage!

Programs Mentioned

Cars — Maths in Motion
Expedition to Saqqara
Front Page Extra
Mary Rose
Newsroom Extra
Police — Language in Evidence
1665
Suburban Fox
Wagons West

References

Bleach, P. (1986) *The Potential of Computers to Aid Understanding*, University of Reading.

DES (1978) *The Primary Survey*, London, HMSO.

DES (1988) *Report of the Committee of Inquiry into the Teaching of English Language*, (The Kingman Report), London, HMSO.

Hampshire (1988) *Computers in the Primary Curriculum*, Hampshire Education Authority, unpublished report.

Walton, D. (1983) 'Education and the New Technology', in Galton, M. and Moon, B. (Eds) *Changing Schools ... Changing Curriculum*, London, Harper and Row.

8   Project Work: Handling Information

David Cowell

There are very many different labels for Integrated Studies in primary education, and the most common ones are identified by Monica Hughes at the beginning of Chapter 5. All of the terms are currently used to describe very similar work being carried out in schools but, for the purposes of this chapter, the term 'project' will be used. Following discussion of some general aspects of such work, a Local Study is described during which the children acquired a relatively deep knowledge of their community, developed a number of important concepts and practised a wide range of skills.

Why Use a Project for the Basis for Learning?

The project helps children to develop skills and to understand concepts in a meaningful and relevant context and gives them an interest in human affairs, and the consideration of the values and attitudes of others will help them develop a value system of their own. This framework also gives children the opportunity to compare their lives, times, culture and environment with those of others, and new insights and experiences can be gained from different subject disciplines used with the 'Project' area.

Concepts

The key concepts that are of paramount importance in any Local Studies project are as follows:

similarity and difference   **communication**
values and beliefs   **conflict and consensus**

continuity and change **causes and consequences**
stewardship and **power**
interdependence

The use of information technology can and does improve the power of these concepts. It enables the child to build a wider, more detailed and tangible picture and to ask the questions 'who, what, why or how?' with the certainty of obtaining a rapid and coherent answer. This allows the child to explore the available information in greater depth.

Skills

Whilst identifying a full range of skills that a 'Local Studies' project might encompass, it is important to understand that only some of these skills will be used in any given project. The choice of skills to be used will influence the approach to, and the organization of the project by the teacher.

Central to the following project outline is the use of an information retrieval package. Rather than prescribe the package to be used, the ideas put forward are of a general nature, therefore whichever piece of software is available the suggestions will be transferable. The most important aspect of this is that the software package is appropriate to the needs and abilities of the children concerned. Ideally, a school should have a progressive range of content-free software such as text-handling packages, databases, and art/design programs. This collection of programs is often referred to as a software toolbox, and examples of suitable databases are DATASHOW, OUR-FACTS and OURSELVES, which are mentioned in Chapter 3. For older or more experienced children the choice would include GRASS, KEY and QUEST. It is extremely important for the teacher to become familiar with the particular software which is going to be used, and the first source of information is the documentation which accompanies such programs. Most contain a sample file of information which can be investigated in order to try out the procedures. Perhaps the most effective way of becoming familiar with a program is to try it out in private, and then talk through any difficulties with a more experienced user. Many programs share similar routines, so the skills acquired in data handling are usually transferable from one program to another, which is a further reason for introducing children to progressively more sophisticated software. The skills which children can develop through the use of these data-handling packages include:

classifying and sorting information,
devising ways of coding information,
collecting and recording information in a logical way,
validating the accuracy of the information,
framing suitable enquiry methods,
choosing the appropriate format for the information
    they require (list form, or graphical representation).

An indication of the skills involved in seven curriculum areas

What is important is that the information is directly relevant to them.

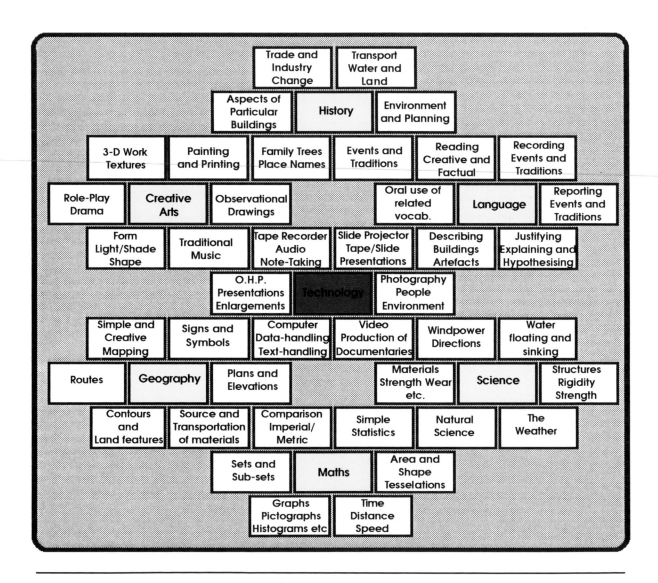

Case Study: A Local Studies Project: Age Range 9–11

Preparation

All the data from the 1881 local census material were entered into an information retrieval package and saved for further use as the project progressed. A subset of records of children under the age of 15 were then taken from the main file and used as the introduction to the children (this information was entered by the teacher), the total number of records in the subset being 100. Using a restricted number of records makes it very easy to talk and explore the file in terms of percentages. From the file a printed list was produced and a copy made for each child, but at this stage not given out.

At the start of the project each child was given a name from the records and asked to imagine who this person was. What did they like? Where did they come from? Did they have a family? They were then asked to write a short imaginary profile of the person. Once these were completed, small sketches of each subject were drawn to complete the record of each imaginary dossier.

During the following days the children typed up their written work using a simple word-processor, and each file was given a reference code related to the author and the subject, e.g. Sam-Tom. This was important as it enabled the need for disc management to be discussed.

Introducing the Data Base

The children were then introduced to the software package using the subset file. Questions were posed for small groups to work on. What percentage of the children on file are male/female? What percentage are under 11 years old? How many children in the file have the same name? What was the most popular name? What seemed to be the least popular name?

From the information gathered, the children were then asked to produce various types of graphical representations. Names within the class were compared against the file of records.

Further questions were asked of each class member for the third session. For example: What did the father of (?) do for a living? How many people were in the family? Where did the parents of (?) come from?

At this point the children were introduced to the complete file of census records from the school area, some 550 in number.

Once further information about each initial subject had been gathered, family portraits were drawn relating to the sort of life style the children thought their original subject had lived, judgements of this kind being directly related to the occupation of the head of the family. The word-processed files were now also amended to incorporate the additional information gathered. The children at this stage appreciated the fact that the work did not have to be re-written, just re-composed. Round one to technology! A follow-up to this activity was for each child to construct his or her own family tree.

Mapwork

The next stage of the project introduced street maps of the locality and copies of the original census material. This proved to be quite an eye-opener for the children. The standard of handwriting on the forms was not good to say the least. Many remarks were made about this and gave a good chance for the children to see the importance of their own skills in this field. At this stage each group of children was asked to locate on the map the addresses of the families in the data file, with the present-day maps being compared to the earliest map of the area available which dated from 1905.

All new additions to the maps were discussed at length for possible reasons for change and a 3D model of the area was also constructed based on the early map. (This has since become a valuable school resource for other teachers.) Buildings of interest and their uses then became the focus of attention. (The first building to be used as a school is now a gift shop.) Observational drawings of building details and special features were undertaken.

Reference Skills — Primary and Secondary Sources

Reference material from the local library was examined in great depth for influential people of the period who were, if possible, located on the database. In one case a fairly well known historical engineer was discovered in the file aged 19, father's occupation 'Blacksmith'. This led on to another small project within the main study. This in fact happened several times with people or buildings.

Many of the children involved in the project started to bring stories about certain areas gleaned from grandparents who provided first-hand information about characters, buildings, families, and so on. This information was useful but not readily usable. It was decided at this point to invite some of these people into the classroom to be interviewed by some of the pupils. Tape recordings were made of the interviews and at a later stage transcripts made on the word-processor, and this provided another valuable resource for future use.

Many of the stories related could be checked in the local newspaper archives. This was done, and other people from our database came to light, even if it was only a mention of their marriage or a birth in the family, or in some cases their death. One such article reported the facts of an accident to a young child who had been run over by a brewer's dray, which led to another mini-project on the means of transport, plus another data file on family cars.

One group explored the possible uses for waste ground found on the map of the area. A visit to one of the plots with outline planning permission yielded a wonderland of insects and their hosts, the wild flowers, and again a mini-project grew out of this visit. The children constructed another data file related to the distribution of the plants in this area. This entailed learning about and devising a means of reference so that each plant could be readily identified in its own position on the plot. Careful watch was kept on the plants, and observations included the species of insect which visited each plant and so on. Accurate drawings were made of the plants *in situ*, and the work of botanical artists was scrutinized with great enthusiasm. The local war memorial also yielded many interesting facts, not simply the names in themselves, and the discussion that followed raised issues that could be debated.

Questionnaires

An interested group of children looked into the trades and occupations of the day. Trade directories were examined and a small group of shops near the school studied for change of use. Comparisons of use were studied in 1881, 1930 and 1986. Shopping patterns were discussed and a visit was planned to the local out-of-town supermarket, which yielded more information. Before the visit the children were asked to construct a data-gathering sheet on which to capture information from the shoppers. All questions asked needed a yes or no answer. Framing the question correctly proved to be a very valuable exercise in the precision of language. As certain interest groups had evolved within the class it was decided to have a three-part form. A small example of the questionnaire is given below.

Shops and Trades Project

	Yes	No
1) Do you shop here often?		
1a) Do you also shop in town?		
2) Did you drive to the shop?		
3) Did you drive less than 15 miles?		
4) Did you drive less than 10 miles?		
5) Did you drive less than 5 miles?		

If the person being questioned had driven to the supermarket then the following question became operable.

Transport Project

1) How long have you been driving? .... **Years**
2) Have you ever had an accident.......................
3) Whose fault was it? Yours, Another's, Road conditions?

The third section of the questionnaire dealt with types of houses: type of dwelling, number of rooms, number of people living in the house, type of heating and insulation. Of the 100 people interviewed only one person refused the children the information required.

All the information was entered into our database and subjected to a fair amount of questioning. Again graphs were produced, but this time through use of the statistical part of the software which enabled histograms and pie-charts to be quickly and easily produced.

Conclusion

The above description of the project is only a thumb-nail sketch of what actually happened, and it is important to remember that it all started with a file on a simple data-base program. The diagram below is an attempt to outline the broad areas covered by the project for the duration of one term. The final production to complete the project was a selection of writing and information about the locality as researched and discovered by the children. Selections were made from the vast number of word-processed files which had been created during the project, and

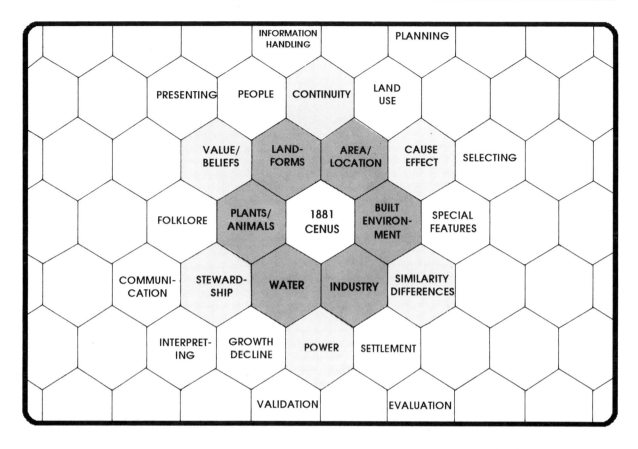

The project involved many key concepts and skills

these were in turn fed into a simple desk-top publishing package, printed and published as a permanent record of the children's work which not only celebrated their achievements but provided tangible evidence of the breadth and depth of the project. For these children, information technology had played an important role in their motivation, their acquisition of skills, and their developing understanding of the locality.

Programs Mentioned

Datashow
Grass
Key
Ourfacts
Ourselves
Quest

9   Problem Solving

Howard Gillings and David Griffiths

The phrase 'Problem Solving' seems to have become very popular of late, but the idea is not new. The Hadow Report in 1931 stated:

> The curriculum of the primary school should be thought of in terms of activity and experience rather than of knowledge to be acquired and facts to be stored.

However, it was the Cockcroft Report in 1982 which discussed problem-solving processes and brought the phrase to the fore:

> Not a great deal is known about the ways in which these problem solving processes develop nor are suitable materials for teachers available. There is a need for more study of children's problem solving activities and of the extent to which strategies for problem solving can be taught.

Virtually all HMI and Schools Council reports point to four major deficiencies in primary school practice. These can be summarized as follows:

1. Brighter pupils are often given undemanding work.
2. Children are given few opportunities for problem-solving activities and few opportunities to apply basic skills in new situations.
3. Pupils are rarely asked to use higher-order thinking skills such as inference, deduction, analysis or evaluation.
4. Except on the games field there is little true group work where pupils can develop the social skills of cooperation and communication.

   The computer can act as a tool for presenting a specific problem or it can provide an environment for more general problem solving. It can also handle the management and presentation of information. Two areas which illustrate the role that the computer can play are 'Turtle Mathematics' and 'Control Technology'.

Turtle Mathematics

The computing language LOGO and its inventor Seymour
Papert have frequently featured in the educational press over the
past few years. We will investigate this language further a little
later in this chapter, but first let us look at the impact that a
children's toy had on the primary classroom.

Programming BigTrak

Big Trak was originally designed as a controllable futuristic
tank. It also had the ability to pull a tippable cart and the
television advertising showed this being programmed by a child
to take an apple to 'Dad'. In my, and many other parents'
experience the novelty soon wore off and the beast was
consigned to a cupboard. However, the resourcefulness of the
good primary teacher had been overlooked. It became apparent
that here was an excellent device for problem-solving activities.

Although it is no longer in production Big Trak can still be
seen in many Primary classrooms. Many attempts have been
made to design an alternative, and recently David Catlin of

A quartet of 'turtles': top left
'Compurobot II' by Systema; bottom
left 'Peter K Bot' by Systema; top
right BigTrak (no longer available);
bottom right 'Valiant Turtle' by
Valiant Technology Ltd

The new 'Roamer' floor turtle is
likely to prove very popular, not least
because of its various disguises

Valiant Technology has produced 'Roamer' which has taken the 'Big Trak' concept much further. The military appearance of the original toy has been replaced by an anonymous robot whose personality can be adapted either by using specially prepared kits or by the imaginative use of cardboard and Blu-tack.

Initial work, however, does not need to involve a machine at all. The teacher, or a child, can program groups of children to move about an area according to the verbal instructions that they receive. An ideal area for this is a Hall with a tiled floor, as the tiles give the basis for accurate measurement of distance. The children are given simple instructions such as

'Forward three (tiles)' or
'Turn left'.

The idea of turning through a measured amount is complex and can involve a great deal of discussion. Initially it is easier if right angles are used, with children turning on the spot to face a new row of tiles.

Later the idea of half-turns, of 45 degrees, can be introduced and the children can use the diagonals of the squares. After simple beginnings things can be made more complex and demanding by putting out obstacles — boxes, tables or stage blocks can be put down to block the direct route from a marked start to a marked finish.

Emphasis can be placed on elegant solutions, 'Who can get to the end in the least number of moves.'

Primary INSET — mep

BIG TRAK

The Big Trak keyboard

Work of this nature involves the children in planning, predicting and testing. It also involves measurement and the use of numbers.

As an extension of this work a robot such as Big Trak or Roamer is programmed to perform a particular task or circum-navigate a particular maze. The robot has a limited 'memory' and so the program can be run, modified if necessary and then re-run. Children learn a great deal from using this machine, and also get a great deal of enjoyment from the exercises. My office is at the end of a corridor and Big Trak has visited me on many occasions. The beast is easily recognized by its characteristic 'drone' and its visits often culminate in the use of its laser cannon! In many schools the machine has been disguised by judicious use of fur fabric and cardboard. Mice, cats and alien beings drone their way around many teaching areas and Halls.

I visited one primary school where the reading scheme 'One, Two, Three and Away' was in use. The teacher had made models of various houses featured in the books and the children had to program the robot to visit the different characters in the stories. A great deal of planning was involved, and in common with all problem-solving activities the children's use of language was remarkable.

Sending BigTrak off to visit the Village with Three Corners

Along similar lines the MEP produced a pack of Big Trak work cards as part of their in-service package entitled 'Posing and Solving Problems with Logo' (this should be available in all Local Authorities). An example of these cards is shown opposite and relates to language work. On card 5 programming Big Trak to spell out ABRACADABRA is a real exercise of planning!

Many teachers have developed number tracks which work in similar ways to the word tracks. Children have to program Big Trak to go to particular numbers and arithmetic signs to form a sum — these can also be quite taxing!

Concrete work of this type can lead to work with computer programs which also fit into the 'problem-solving' category. A

bigtrak

Primary INSET

You will need: Bigtrak

a very large piece of paper

and a pencil

a friend to work with

Draw this crossroads on a piece of paper, or on the playground if your teacher says you may.

```
                    B
                    
   A        R         C
                    
                    D
```

Write programs to make Bigtrak go from **A** to **B**

from **A** to **C**

Which was easier?

Can you program Bigtrak to spell **BAD** or **CAB** ?

Now spell **ABRACADABRA !**

natural progression from free-standing robots is to Turtle Graphics programs. Turtle Graphics is a subset of the language Logo. This powerful programming language was developed by Seymour Papert and the subtitle gives an insight into its content — 'Children, Computers and Powerful Ideas'. The full language involves much more than Turtle Graphics with complex list handling routines, but the misnomer 'Logo' is often applied to the work with Turtle Graphics carried out in schools. The program's rather strange name comes from the shape of the 'screen pointer' in Papert's original — it was shaped like a turtle,

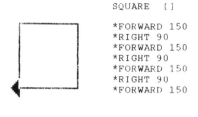

```
SQUARE   []

*FORWARD 150
*RIGHT 90
*FORWARD 150
*RIGHT 90
*FORWARD 150
*RIGHT 90
*FORWARD 150
```

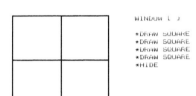

```
WINDOW [ ]

*DRAW SQUARE
*DRAW SQUARE
*DRAW SQUARE
*DRAW SQUARE
*HIDE
```

```
HEXAGON []

*REPEAT 6
* FORWARD 150
* RIGHT 60
* END REPEAT
```

with the 'head' showing which way the pointer was facing. Subsequent versions of the program often use a simpler triangle but still retain the title Turtle Graphics. There are many such packages, but one which combines the best features of most is DELTA which was developed by teachers in Berkshire. The illustrations in this chapter were produced using this program.

Using a programming language of this kind requires the use of simple procedures. These individual procedures are combined to make the complete program. Let us take a simple program to draw a 'window' as an example. This shape is best thought of as four squares joined together. The initial procedure would be one to draw a single square, another would then combine four squares (each drawn by the same procedure) to form the final picture.

Producing even the simple square shape needs the child to have grasped certain concepts — mainly those of right angles and equal length. Using the quite simple syntax illustrated the child can manipulate the 'turtle' around the screen, leaving a track when required.

Allowing children to explore, to formulate ideas — try them, modify them, and then try again — enables them to 'discover' what (for example) a square really is. The old saying 'I do and I understand' really applies in work like this.

Papert felt very strongly that the child should find all the answers without adult help but in most classroom situations we would find the teacher on hand to 'ask the right questions' and guide the child forward in the process of discovery.

As skills develop, children find that many of their procedures contain repeated sections and they begin to refine their programs to use repeat loops and other sophisticated programming tools. The use of these arises from their own needs and perceptions, and in this way they learn the real power of the language.

An extension of the work with Turtle Graphics on a monitor screen can be to use a floor turtle. This is a device controlled by the computer which can move around the floor and leave pen traces on a large sheet of paper. Some models are connected directly to the computer by an umbilical cord, but the 'Valiant Turtle' is controlled by a special infra-red interface which plugs into the computer. By using this system, which is similar to the remote control used for television sets, the wires joining turtle to computer are dispensed with. This solves the problem of tangling, and also gives the turtle a 'magic' quality. The floor turtle obeys the same commands as the screen turtle and the 'pen down' and 'pen up' commands control a felt tip pen inserted into a holder on the base of the machine. A turtle of this nature enables very large designs to be made.

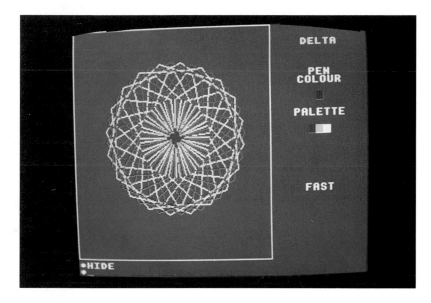

Children delight in producing patterns such as this, and develop mathematical concepts at the same time

Control Technology

With the development of Craft, Design and Technology in schools the computer has begun to be used to control and animate the models and projects involved. The basic requirements for this are:

Computer interface
Sensors
Output devices — motors, bulbs, etc.
A suitable control program.

Computer Interface

This is a 'black box' which acts as a buffer between the computer and the controlled devices. The electronics inside this box ensure that no damage can come to the computer and give the computer output the necessary power to operate the devices. There are several of these interfaces available from suppliers, and many local authorities, for example Barnet, Brent and Berkshire, have produced their own. Sockets are provided

The Berkshire control box (left) and an interface produced by Micrex

on the box to enable the easy connection of both sensors and output devices. The box will either take its power directly from the computer or have a built in power supply and plug into a mains socket.

Sensors

These provide a means of asserting certain conditions which the program can use in controlling the output devices. Sensors can be light-sensitive, magnetic switches, temperature switches or even simple contact switches. They can be used in many ways, perhaps to sense whether a door is open or closed, perhaps to sense if a beam of light has been broken.

Output Devices

These are the bits and pieces actually operated by the computer through the control program. These could be motors, light bulbs or any device which can be controlled through the interface. In this way robots can be made to move and traffic lights operated in the correct sequence.

Control Program

This is the software which enables the computer to 'read' the sensors and operate the output devices. It is possible to do this through the standard programming language BASIC. However, this requires a sound knowledge of the language, and BASIC is not really designed for this purpose. It is much better, and considerably easier, to use a specific control program. Many of these programs exist, but some of the easiest types are those based around the LOGO language. A good example of a control logo is CONTACT from MESU. Being logo-based, each program is built up from simple procedures, and the programmer does not need to know difficult syntax as much of the language is similar to English.

Using the correct equipment controlling a model is not really difficult. The main problem is in identifying exactly what is required and sequencing each action in a logical way. Children respond very well to this type of problem solving and are capable of making the most marvellous machines and models.

Tackling the problem and sharing ideas

A group of third and fourth year children in a small Berkshire school illustrate how control can be used. Using the county control box and its associated input and output devices the children were given a simple electric train set with assorted buildings and asked to design a traffic light and safety system. The children built up a simple oval track with a station and level crossing. They decided that they needed to ensure that no train could enter the station if another was already there and also that the level crossing would not operate if there was a vehicle stranded on it. These children had a good basic knowledge of writing simple procedures through using the delta Turtle Graphics program and did not find the CONTACT package too difficult (the teacher only gave assistance on one or two occasions). Working together for a full afternoon the children developed a layout where the signals indicated if the station was occupied and the computer itself showed if there was a vehicle on the level crossing. Both of these used light sensors as detectors and the children were only prevented from actually isolating an oncoming train in times of danger by the lack of suitable relay (electrically controlled switch). The whole after-noon was most impressive and later in the week the children brought in to school some of their own equipment and developed the layout further.

Problem-solving activities provide an ideal opportunity for children to apply basic skills. They also encourage the processes of hypothesis, testing, analysis and evaluation. The two example areas outlined in this chapter are only part of what can be done. Many problem-solving programs exist in their own rights, and I can only encourage you to try them ... and watch the children GO!

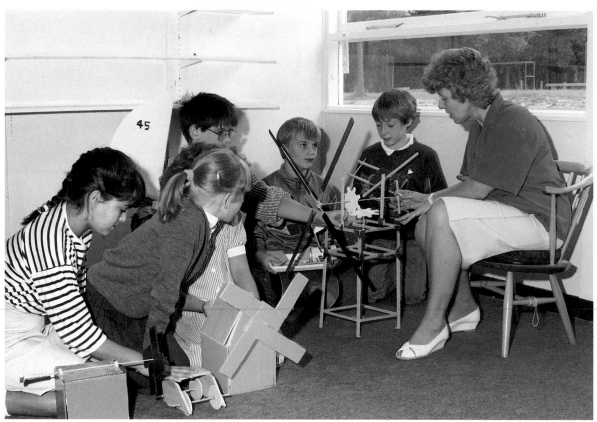

Discussing the solutions

Programs mentioned

Contact
Delta

References

Cockcroft Report (1982) *Mathematics Counts, Report of the Committee of Inquiry into the teaching of Mathematics in Schools*, London, HMSO.
Hadow Report (1931) *Report of the Consultative Committee on Primary Schools*, London, HMSO.
MEP (1986) *Posing and Solving Problems with the Micro*, MEP.
Papert, S. (1980) *Mindstorms*, London, Harvester Press.

10 Beyond the QWERTY Keyboard

Chris Hopkins

The numerous ways in which the computer can enhance the curriculum in primary schools are identified throughout this book and there are many suggestions about the ways particular programs can be used. There are however a number of problems which may confront children when using a computer in the classroom.

The keyboard has an unusual arrangement of the alphabet which means that children often spend time looking for the letters they want.

The keys are in upper case whereas the children are used to lower case and this can lead to confusion and in some classrooms to teachers sticking lower case labels onto the keys.

The child has to type in whole words which, sometimes, have to be correctly spelt before the program moves on.

In some programs individual keys are used to represent words, phrases or actions, involving the child in the need to remember what stands for what. How much better if the letters could be in an easily remembered sequence; if whole words could be entered at once simply by pressing the word; if pictures could be used as cues or to represent ideas.

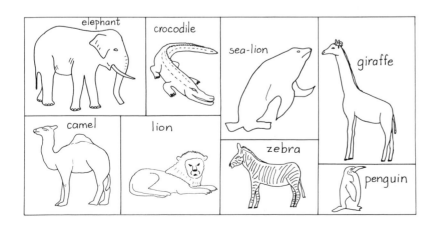

All this is possible with a Concept Keyboard because on it you can have exactly what you want the children to see, be that letters (upper or lower case), words, pictures, symbols or objects. If the topic is 'The Zoo' there can be a colourful overlay with pictures of various zoo animals on it.

The overlays do not have to be restricted to pictures. A room in a house can be depicted by carpet and dolls' house furniture. Overlays can be made using 'Press and Peel' sheets or 'fuzzy felt' giving the pupils the opportunity to move the objects on the overlay around. The overlay will change as it is being used.

Such possibilities expand the use of the computer with children of all ages and abilities.

But what is a Concept Keyboard?

A Concept Keyboard is a pressure-sensitive board, usually A3 or A4 in size. It plugs into the user port, which is on the underside of the computer, next to the printer port. Pressure on the Concept Keyboard sends a signal to the computer. The keyboard is divided into an 8 by 16 grid, giving 128 differently sensitive sections. This means that the computer can 'recognize' which area of the Concept Keyboard has been pressed and react accordingly.

An attractive overlay featuring the delightful PODD

The way in which it reacts depends upon the program being used at the time. In some programs all the areas will react in exactly the same way, so the Concept Keyboard acts as a single switch, which is effectively how the QWERTY keyboard behaves with programs that only use the space bar. In others, different squares or groups of squares will react in different ways, depending on the program. A press on an area of the Concept Keyboard could cause the computer to react as if a single key on the QWERTY keyboard had been pressed, or a single press could cause the production of up to six lines of text.

As far as the pupils are concerned the Concept Keyboard is simply another way of interacting with the computer. The 8 by 16 grid is hidden by the overlay in use, which provides them with visually stimulating information and an easy way to interact with the computer.

Initially the potential of the Concept Keyboard was seen for children with special needs and it was into that area that it went first. Consequently the software that was developed was for children with learning difficulties. Gradually, and partly due to the development of 'framework' (or 'content-free') programs, the Concept Keyboard is being recognized as a useful tool in many more classrooms. It can be used successfully in the nursery and the secondary classroom and across the ability range.

For children in the early stages of reading and writing the Concept Keyboard provides the facility to enter whole words into the text and to have pictures on the overlay as cues. All of this means that stories can be written without the child having to concentrate on holding the pencil and shaping the letters or having to search around the QWERTY keyboard to find the letters. 'I recognize that word. That's the one I want.'

The computer can be used in a 'Breakthrough' fashion with programs such as FREEWRITER and PROMPT/WRITER, the overlay having on it the words the child knows. This links the process of reading and writing. With the additional aid of a speech synthesizer, the child can explore the overlay, listen to the word and decide whether or not that is the one she/he wants. It enables the child to discover new words. With FREEWRITER the words known by the child are highlighted on the overlay, but if there are other words on the overlay, some exploration and discovery is possible. It is also possible to add new words to the overlay as they are needed and learned by the child.

yes / no	why / because	what / when	big / bad	happy / new	picture story	baby	am / is	have / has	read / write	...ed / ...ing	by / on	
I / you	we / they	she / he	little / good		mum / dad	cat / dog	boy / girl	are / was	will / were	run / jump	... s / ...es	out / at	
him / her	me / my	it	pretty / naughty		shop / car	brother / sister		be / been	want / said	skip / watch	...n't	to / in	speak
a / the	this / that	some / all	birthday party		home		with / of	do / did	go / went	kiss / cry	love / like	down / up	
here / there	lot	very / not	children / friend		school / teacher		and / but	make / made	came / come	play / walk	work / paint	? / .	new page
time	book / house		yesterday / today		morning / night		after / for	had / can	see / saw	sit / sleep	get / got	!	rubber
													new line

A typical FREEWRITER overlay

The use of green and blue highlights makes it possible for there to be up to 200 words on the overlay, allowing a fairly large vocabulary bank to be built up. The overlay could have on it the words of the current reading book of the child. This gives the child the opportunity to encounter the words in a different context and to manipulate them into stories of his/her own. Additional cues can be given on the overlay such as differently coloured words and pictures as well as, or instead of, words.

The use of the Concept Keyboard with a word-processor does not preclude the use of the QWERTY keyboard. As the child's writing and word-processing skills develop, the use of the QWERTY and Concept Keyboards can be combined, the Concept Keyboard having on it, for example, lots of descriptive words to stimulate imagination or special topic words not commonly in use. Often, when using overlays with large numbers of descriptive words on them, not only are those words used but also others that are not there. This is because, in the process of selecting the most appropriate word, others spring to mind and there is the security of having a variety of words all known to be spelt correctly. The immediate thought is not, therefore, 'I might use .... or .... if I could spell them, but I can't, so I'll use "nice"!'

A group discussion on the language of a particular topic can create a word list. This can then very easily be turned into an overlay for use during the course of the topic work. When working in a specific subject area it is often useful to have the technical terms on the overlay, acting as reminders and speeding up the writing, as a single press enters the word or phrase with no spelling mistakes.

The Concept keyboard plugs into the 'user port' underneath the computer

For some children with a physical handicap the computer has made an enormous difference to their ability to write and express themselves. The child who could not hold a pencil can manage to manipulate a keyboard or Concept Keyboard. Additional aids may well be necessary. If the hand finds it difficult to locate particular keys or areas, without others being inadvertently pressed, then a keyguard or Concept Keyboard

A keyguard being used over the QWERTY keyboard

can be used. The keys are effectively recessed, making accidental pressing less likely, while finding what is wanted.

It is also possible to obtain expanded keyboards which not only recess the keys but make it possible for a time and repeat delay to be set so a key has to be deliberately held for a certain time before it is accepted and there is a delay before the letter is repeated on the screen.

For children with limited movement and reach it is also possible to obtain mini keyboards, miniaturised versions of the ordinary keyboard, giving them access to the power of the computer. Both mini and expanded keyboards can be interfaced with the BBC computers, so that either the conventional or the new keyboard can be used.

'Content-free' software like PROMPT/WRITER comes with a number of sample overlays, which give ideas of the ways in which the program can be used and the sorts of overlays that can be created. However, to make the best of the program, teachers will want to create overlays that relate specifically to the children in their classroom.

The making of an overlay is not a complicated process. The programs that use them provide clear and simple on-screen instructions and frequently check that you did what you wanted to do, thereby giving the opportunity to correct the odd spelling mistake or the pressing of the wrong part of the Concept Keyboard. The most important and difficult part of making a worksheet is not writing it out but deciding upon its content and layout, and the same is true of a Concept Keyboard overlay. Once it is designed, sitting down and typing the information in is very straightforward.

Many programs make excellent use of the Concept Keyboard, without the need to have overlays made for them.

MOVING IN, a program for use in the lower school classroom, comes with a choice of two overlays. The child or group of children is presented with an empty house which has to be filled with furniture by typing sentences such as

Put the bath in the bathroom

This can be done from the QWERTY keyboard but it can be both very time-consuming and frustrating when a single typing error means the computer doesn't 'understand'. The program comes into its own when used with the Concept Keyboard. The overlay has on it the words needed for the sentence construction, arranged from left to right on the overlay. There are pictures of the furniture alongside the words so they can be recognized easily. The children have a lot of fun, furnishing their house, moving the furniture around, changing beds into chairs or people into plants, whilst at the same time developing both reading and writing skills. (The program can be set so that it will not accept syntactically incorrect sentences.)

A large number of other activities relating to the home can be continuing alongside this, and programs like PROMPT/ WRITER can be used to write stories about moving house, using overlays based on the MOVING IN overlay.

Moving in

I		ball	cupboard	television	strike	bird in the tree		cloudy
put	a	bath	fire	toilet	in	left	attic	sunny
take away	the	bed	fridge	wardrobe	into	right	bedroom	rainy
change	the	bookcase	piano	Jim	to	middle	bathroom	snowy
make	it	cat	plant	Jane	the	of	living	light
move	the	chair	sink	Julie	from	a	kitchen	dark
we		clock	sofa	wash	have a bath	door open	door close	RETURN
		cooker	table	lie down	play the piano	space	•	RUB OUT

In conjunction with Manchester SEMERC and MESU Special Needs Software Centre

The Concept Keyboard has, as we have seen, the advantage of allowing the input of whole words or phrases. It also has other advantages. When using a program which uses very few keys on the computer keyboard the others can be a distraction and a confusion, which the use of the Concept Keyboard removes. If a group of children are using the computer, often one has the task of keying in the instructions. She/he then has the important place near the screen and often the others can't actually see what she/he is doing. Put the information onto the Concept Keyboard and the 'keys' immediately become larger and more visible, the distractors have been removed and, because it has a fairly long ribbon cable, the Concept Keyboard can often be passed around the group, rather than having one child in charge.

One program that can be used in this way is the music program COMPOSE, a version of which works with the Concept Keyboard and comes complete with overlays. (A full description of this program can be found in Chapter 11.)

Compose

Overlay 2

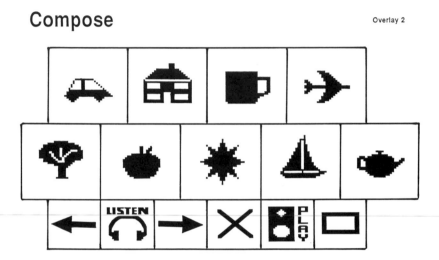

An overlay for COMPOSE

The pictorial phrases can be chosen simply by pressing them. Phrases can be listened to or placed in the music by pressing the correct symbol, which could be anything the children would like. The other children have a clear view of what the person with the keyboard is doing and it is easy to move the Concept Keyboard from one person to another. Teachers could, if they wished, replace the pictures with other symbols on the overlay, for example the notation of the phrase or a pattern of its rhythm.

The use of the Concept Keyboard with the program allows the blind child the opportunity to manipulate the tunes. The pictures can be replaced by shapes and textures.

If numbers of objects are used instead of the pictures, then different tune files can be identified by the different object, for example the button tune or the bead tune, but the position on the overlay will always relate to how many beads, buttons, etc. there are.

It also means that the blind child can more easily contribute with her sighted classmates in the creation of their tune as she

A keyguard being used over a Concept keyboard

too has a picture in her head of the phrase. If she refers to 'phrase 4' the child in charge of the keyboard can easily work out that 'that's the second picture in on the top row', or there could be numbers alongside the pictures, and if someone then comments that that's the 'house', all the children know which picture is being referred to and after a while all the children know which phrase is being referred to.

An expanded keyboard being used by a child with difficulties in controlling movement

There are many ways in which the use of the Concept Keyboard together with a speech synthesizer can benefit the blind or partially-sighted child. The overlay can be a 'feely' one, using raised patterns, objects, cut-out shapes or brailled words. Programs such as PROMPT/WRITER and TOUCH EXPLORER + can be used to great effect.

MESU's Special Needs Software Centre has recently produced CONCEPT, a piece of software which will allow many programs which were originally written for the QWERTY keyboard to be accessed via the Concept Keyboard. In many cases this makes the programs easier for the children to use as they do not have to remember which key stands for what and problems with spelling are overcome.

An example of a program which can now make use of the Concept Keyboard is the infant adventure game LOST FROG. This program, designed as an early introductory adventure game, is one where the children have to remember a number of instructions in their heads and remember how to spell words with which they are not necessarily very familiar. The children have to explore a house, trying to find the frog and release it. During their explorations they come across objects which may be useful some time and they can choose to pick these up and

take them with them. They come across problems such as 'How can I get past the dog and get upstairs?'.

For children using such programs for the first time there is a great deal to take in and remember and the Concept Keyboard frees them of some of these problems. It provides pictorial information. It reminds them which way right and left are. It gives them clues about the things they might find that might be useful and so encourages them to keep looking when they decide something is needed — like a bone for the dog.

They still have to make sure they know where they are in the house and that they have the items they need at the appropriate times. They have to work out which is the item to leave behind when their arms are full as only four things can be carried at any one time. The Concept Keyboard overlay gives additional visual information to the child and so enhances the program.

Concept can be used to create overlays for word-processors such as WORDWISE and INTERWORD, providing the benefits previously mentioned together with a more sophisticated word-processor.

It can also be used to great effect to create overlays that will drive a floor or a screen turtle (see Chapter 9). The overlay can be as simple as or complicated as is required. It can give the child a pictorial representation of the command and removes the necessity of remembering the abbreviations for forwards, backwards, etc. It also means that the pupil can keep watching the floor turtle and not have to turn his back on it to type in the next instruction.

The Concept Keyboard not only provides an easy means of entering information or instructions into the computer, but it can be used equally well as an information provider.

LIST EXPLORER allows the exploration of a pictorial database.

The pupil chooses the child she/he wants to find out about and presses the picture. The child's name appears on the screen. She/he can then choose what she/he wants to know about the child, by pressing, and the information is displayed as requested.

This is a good introduction to databases, linking the use of the Concept Keyboard which is used both to find out information and provide pictures of the items that are being investigated, and the QWERTY keyboard which is used when comparisons between items are being made.

A database of fabrics could have small pieces of each of the materials attached. A floral database could have pictures or

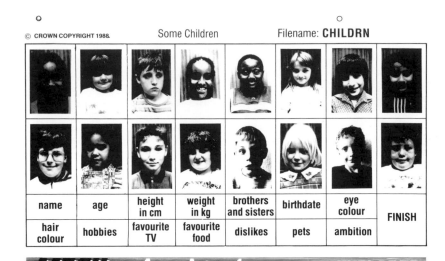

A pictorial data base

children's drawings, making the flowers easier to recognize and remember.

TOUCH EXPLORER + is a program which makes full use of the potential of the Concept Keyboard. At its simplest you just touch the Concept Keyboard to explore. It is the imagination of the teacher and the versatility of the program that enables the effective use of this software right across the age, curriculum and ability range. It is a 'framework' program which comes with a number of sample files indicating some of the ways in which the program could be used.

One such file is 'Elizabethan Cottage'. As you can see the overlay is very simple with very little information on it. This is deliberate as the teacher who designed it did not want to provide her pupils with any preconceived ideas about living in Elizabethan times. Pressing 'Start here' gives the information:

> **Discover what your home would be like if you were a peasant during the reign of Elizabeth I.**
> **For help with words in red, press "Help"**

By pressing the squares of the cottage the pupils begin to build up a mental picture of what life might have been like:

> **This is the wall of your cottage.**
> **It is made of wattle and daub.**
> **It is damp.**
> **Your sister Ann is watching the fleas jumping on the bed.**
> **There is an unpleasant smell here.**

Little Tom hasn't learnt to go to the toilet yet!
A home-made candle stands here.
The smoke escapes through a hole in the roof.
A wooden settle stands against the wall. Mother is very
proud of it.

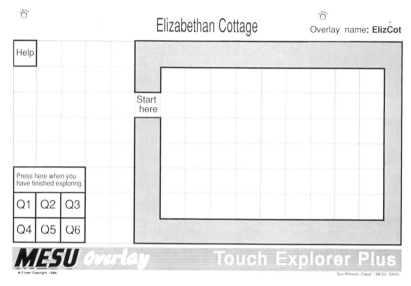

Words like 'settle' and 'wattle and daub' are written in red so pressing 'Help' will provide more information about them. There are then a number of questions and tasks which make the pupils think about the information they have discovered:

What smells could you imagine in the cottage? (You
should have found at least four).
Tell me about Tom.

Notes on the exploration can be made in one of many ways, perhaps the most obvious one being paper and pencil. Symbols could be put on the overlay to indicate where things are. If a printer is attached to the computer then screen messages can be printed out at any time simply by pressing 'P', so pupils can make their notes in that way. All the messages that the pupils look at can be printed, either by setting the program to print out everything as it happens or by choosing to print out the exploration when it is finished. If you haven't got a printer you can save a copy of your exploration and then use it at a later date in PROMPT/WRITER or another word-processor.

It is possible to make notes from within the program itself. (This is possible only if you are running the program on a BBC Master computer). If at any time during an exploration you press 'N' or a notepad square on the overlay you move out of TOUCH EXPLORER + into WRITER taking with you what-ever was on the screen at the time. In this way questions can be taken through to the notepad, the exploration can continue and when answers are found they can be added to the notes. When in the notepad it is also possible to type in any details that are wanted and to move text about as one does in WRITER. The notes can be saved for future use or printed out.

When using the 'Elizabethan Cottage', each square of the Concept Keyboard can hold one message. TOUCH EXPLORER + will allow up to six different messages for any one square. 'Time Tunnel' is an example of an overlay that makes use of this. The pupils are presented with an overlay containing a very diagrammatic picture of King William Street in Blackburn, six different date squares and six question squares. When the overlay is loaded, the date on the screen is 1874.

Pressing one of the houses on the overlay will give informa-tion about the premises:

1874
25 Holt J.
Draper and Silk Merchant

Pressing on the date squares will show what has happened to number 25 over the last century:

1894
25 Lipton T. J.
Provision Merchant
1915
25 Lipton Ltd.
Grocers
1939
25 Scotts Ltd.
Tailors
1960
25 Wilson H. & J. Ltd.
Gowns
1988
25 Abbey National
Building Society

The street can be explored through time, looking at how the use of the buildings has changed, and how and why the occupations have changed. The whole street can be explored for, say, 1939, with the pupils trying to envisage what the street was like fifty years ago. The questions on the overlay give direction to the exploration.

This overlay could be the start of a local investigation, the pupils finding out about their own environment, and developing an awareness of local business and commerce. Present-day information could be collected by pupils directly, a street plan could be drawn and buildings marked on it and possibly photographed.

Old street directories and other archive material could be examined for the earlier details. Pupils could find out about street lighting and transport over the past hundred years. They could create their own Touch Explorer files about their locality for pupils in other years to investigate. The visits to the local high street could be used to glean all sorts of other information. What variety of fruit and vegetables is sold in the greengrocers? Where does it come from? How busy is the street, both in terms of cars and pedestrians?

At a very different level simple files can be created for TOUCH EXPLORER + with pictures on the overlay and single words appearing on the screen. These words can be reinforced or replaced by the use of a speech synthesizer. Separate speech messages can be used with TOUCH EXPLORER + , which means that words the speech synthesizer 'finds difficult' can be rewritten to sound more accurate or spoken and written messages can be different.

A feely overlay

Files can be made to link up with 'Fuzzy Felt', 'Press'n'Peel', or small toys, involving the pupils in creating a scene on the overlay and then using and manipulating it. The sample files are just that, examples to indicate the many exciting ways in which the program can be used. Having 'played' with the program the imaginative teacher will come up with many ideas and will want to create his/her own files to suit the needs of his/her pupils and the work currently being done in the classroom. The Concept Keyboard can add an extra dimension to the use of the computer in the classroom. It is not simply a tool for those who have not yet learnt to type. Used well it can provide a stimulating environment which enhances everything else that is happening in the classroom.

Programs Mentioned

Compose
Concept
Freewriter
Interword
List Explorer
Lost Frog
Moving In
Prompt/Writer
Touch Explorer +
Wordwise Plus

For details of suppliers of specialist keyboards, keyguards and speech synthesizers see Appendix A.

11 Creative Activities: Music

David Congdon

Computers have had an association with music for many years, some of the early valve computers having been used by various serious composers as a basis for composition. With the advent of the microcomputer it has become possible for a wider range of people to have access to computer-generated sounds, and despite the BBC computer's limited sound capabilities (four fairly basic sound channels), it does offer some interesting possibilities for the musician. Perhaps more significantly for the class teacher, the non-musician can provide extremely worthwhile musical activities for children.

Software

Although immediate possibilities were offered by the BBC micro, it has taken a long time for anything really impressive, and, more particularly, useful to the primary-age child, to come along. Many of the programs have merely imitated aspects of music that can just as easily be carried out by more traditional methods, and, though fun, failed to make an original use of the computer.

The aims of music education contained in the DES guidelines for music from 5 to 16 tell us that 'Music education should be mainly concerned with bringing children into contact with the musician's fundamental activities of performing, composing and listening.' Many music teachers, especially non-specialists at the primary level, find the composition part of this aim to be difficult to achieve with the limited knowledge they themselves have.

What was needed was a program that enables the child to compose at the computer, but without making the task too complicated.

'Music education should be mainly concerned with bringing children into contact with the musician's fundamental activities of performing, composing and listening' (Music, 5–16)

COMPOSE

A program that does offer a great deal to children of a wide age range and ability is COMPOSE, written by Andy Pierson. With its quick and easy method of producing original compositions, and its simple but effective graphics, it is of immense appeal to children.

The program allows the child to select from up to nine musical phrases, or snippets of tunes, each of which is represented by a picture. The user can listen to each one in turn, then arrange them on the screen in the order they wish, to make their own piece. On playback the individual melodic cells are chained together to make a piece. It's as simple as that!

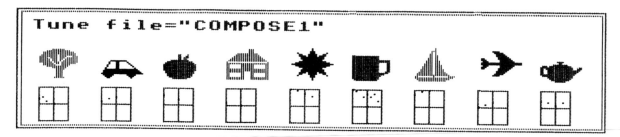

To explain the idea another way, an analogy can be drawn to Language. Imagine writing a story by choosing from a number of phrases rather than individual words. Some of the phrases make good beginnings, others make good ends, but all of them will fit together because they are written that way. Imagine in addition being able to press a button and hear the story being read back to you. This would be a quick, easy and exciting way of writing a story. COMPOSE operates in this way, with musical phrases being chosen instead of individual notes. As COMPOSE allows you to choose from sections of musical melody, rather than the separate notes, the results are much quicker, and a successful composition is almost guaranteed, an important factor particularly with younger children.

On the face of it one might assume that all pieces produced with COMPOSE would sound the same; however, this is not necessarily the case. As each musical phrase/picture is chosen there are nine choices for the next (the same one again or any of the eight others), and as this is repeated at each step, the range of possibilities is vast.

In addition to the tune file (set of phrases and pictures) that is normally loaded in, the user can select from a wide range of additional tune files, giving a much greater variation in the styles of music that can be produced. There is for instance a tune file in Chinese pentatonic style, an Egyptian one, a minor one and so on. Once the children have mastered the first (and most basic) one, there is a great deal of scope for further composition.

What really makes COMPOSE so impressive, though, is the

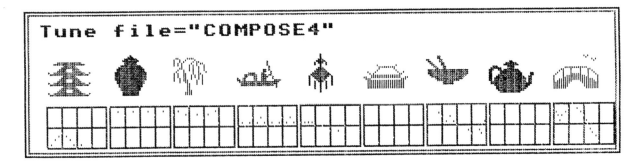

versatility of the programming, allowing a high degree of control over many aspects of the music and graphics, and it is this versatility that makes COMPOSE so useful to teachers. Music specialists find it a powerful and versatile tool, non-specialists use it as a convenient, exciting and flexible way of involving composition in class music.

To give some idea of the flexibility, here are some of the other things COMPOSE can do:

The layout and number of pictures on screen can be varied between 1 and 80.

The speed of playback can be altered over a wide range.

Once a tune has been written it can be saved to disc with a suitable name. Up to thirty tunes will fit on a disc, and a catalogue of tunes already on the disc is always given.

The complete piece can also be sent to a printer, giving the children a 'hard copy' of their work.

The tune can be cleared for a fresh start.

The children can select continuous play, where the tune starts again automatically each time it finishes.

All this is achieved with a minimum of key presses, with all of the important functions requiring only single keys. Frequent use is made of messages checking whether you want to continue with a particular command, which avoids having to go through with a course of action you did not mean to take. A number of useful help pages can also be called up in different parts of the program, making it very easy to use without constant resort to the manual.

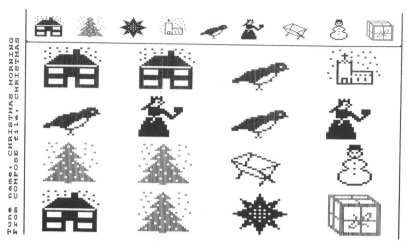

A printout of 'Christmas morning'

'Christmas Morning' with graphics by the children and musical phrases by the teacher

Without doubt the most versatile part of the software is the Editor. Though COMPOSE can be used successfully without ever going near the Editor, it allows the creative teacher to tailor the program to a specific project or activity. Using the Editor, the on-screen pictures can be swapped around or edited, or new ones can be drawn. The tune files themselves can be printed out, swapped, edited, or entirely new ones written from scratch. The possibilities opened up by this are almost endless, and it is this feature that allows the creation of original material. Of the two main sections of the Editor, editing pictures and editing phrases, editing pictures is by far the easiest to use. Even young children can manage to produce their own pictures. As the tune editor is more complicated, it is better suited to older pupils or teachers, although of course a lot will depend on the previous experience of the user.

COMPOSE has a lot to offer in the way of notation (writing music down). The way COMPOSE uses pictures to represent musical phrases is a form of graphic notation, an approach currently favoured in music education. As with any sort of notation, it encourages the children to understand the way that music can be represented in a variety of graphic and pictorial ways. COMPOSE also uses another form of notation which can be found in the Editor. This type is called 'Window Notation' and is a simplified way of writing down the pitch and rhythm of the musical phrases in the tune files. It is a very useful way of identifying the various different tunes when you are using the Editor.

Editing lyrics with PENDOWN

MIDI

One of the problems with the BBC micro is the low volume and relatively poor quality of the internal sound. No matter how good the tune, it is always played by the same type of sound. An important feature of COMPOSE is the ability to play its tunes through an electronic keyboard or synthesizer. This improves dramatically the quality of sound, and introduces an entirely new dimension to composing, that of being able to select the type of sound or instrument that you want your tune to be played on. Since most synthesizers also allow you to play on the keyboard at the same time, it means you can add another part as the computer plays your tune.

The information is passed from the computer to the keyboard via MIDI, which stands for Musical Instrument Digital Interface. MIDI is a system, agreed by all the major manufacturers, that allows computers and electronic keyboards to be linked together. The COMPOSE program sends out the appropriate information as it is playing the tune back. Unfortunately the BBC micro is not built with a MIDI interface, so a separate box containing the interface has to be connected between the computer and the synthesizer. Only two connections need to be made to the computer, both to sockets underneath, adjacent to the printer and disc drive connectors. A single DIN lead then runs from the 'MIDI out' on the interface box to the 'MIDI in' on the synthesizer.

Only certain synthesizers are capable of receiving MIDI information. Those that are normally have a pair of DIN-type sockets, labelled 'MIDI in' and 'MIDI out'. However, most keyboards are MIDI-compatible now, and the facility is gradually appearing on more low-priced keyboards.

All this extra equipment needed to produce the improved sound doesn't come cheap! The recommended MIDI interface, manufacturered by EMR Ltd, and a keyboard capable of receiving the MIDI information, would require an expenditure which would be difficult to justify if it were to support just one computer program. However, if the school is considering buying a keyboard for classroom music etc., it is certainly worth ensuring it is MIDI-compatible, so that it can be used with the program. The MIDI interface itself would only then need to be purchased. Another important point is that COMPOSE is not the only program to make use of MIDI. Other programs are available now, and more will be in the future, that make creative use of the MIDI interface. Some of these programs are mentioned at the end of this chapter. With the MIDI facility gradually appearing on keyboards at the cheaper end of the market, the cost of setting up a system will eventually be much less, and, for the quality of sound available, it is certainly worth considering.

Improvising with a self-composed tune. Note the MIDI interface to the right of the computer

Using COMPOSE in the Classroom

COMPOSE is such a powerful, versatile program that there are many different ways that it can be used successfully in the primary classroom. It can be used as a 'stand-alone' program, or as part of a project. It can be used as a resource to 'dip into' from time to time, or in a more systematic way. Whichever way is chosen, COMPOSE will always be fun, and in my experience, children are never bored using it!

I was lucky enough to be introduced to COMPOSE by its writer, Andy Pierson, at a one-day course. As a music specialist I was immediately impressed by the software, as was a fellow teacher from the school, himself a non-specialist. What impressed us both was firstly the originality of the idea of composing with pictures where each one represented a musical phrase, and secondly the depth that the program offered, in terms of the variety of styles in the tune files and the comprehensive editing facilities. It seemed that everything you wanted to do was possible and had already been thought of, showing evidence of extensive classroom trials. We left the course firmly hooked on COMPOSE!

COMPOSE ... children are never bored using it!

Since then we have both used the program extensively, with groups of first and second juniors, and with third and fourth years. Other members of staff, including infant teachers, have also become interested and have used the program. We were lucky enough to already have an electronic keyboard with

MIDI capabilities, and so we have always used the program's MIDI facilities.

My own use of the program has been mainly with first and second year juniors, and has taken two different forms. At first I used the program with different groups of children, using an exploratory approach, i.e., the children were encouraged to explore the facilities the program offered, and come up with a piece. I gave them the minimum of input, simply showing them how to load the program, and being on hand to help when needed, and of course to listen to the finished pieces. The children had great fun, wrote some interesting pieces and were obviously making some compositional decisions, e.g. 'The house makes a good ending', or 'The mug doesn't sound right there, try the star'. However there was a great disparity between the level of understanding of different children. Those who were more adventurous and computer-wise had discovered many different parts of the program, tried out new tune files and even the Editor, while others had spent their entire time on Compose 1, the first tune file.

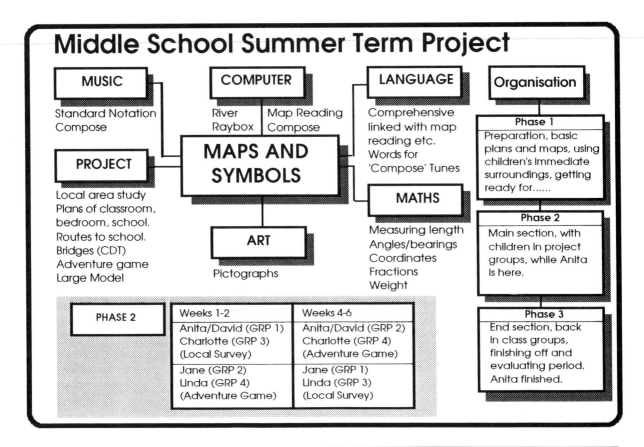

From this initial work I decided that a more systematic approach, where actual targets were given, might be more appropriate, and might result in a better and more consistent level of understanding. The second time I used the program, therefore, I planned for a more progressive acquisition of skills and concepts and, with its heavy emphasis on graphic notation, COMPOSE was the ideal program to provide a musical aspect to a project on 'Maps and Symbols'.

In the first session children were introduced to the program as a class, and were shown the way to select pictures to build up a tune. After this the children were split into groups and set the initial task of composing a short piece. To help with this I prepared a card giving a few hints and reminding them of the most important keys.

The children were all encouraged to save their work, and to make a printout if they wanted. Only when everyone had got to this stage, albeit at their own level, did we progress to the next task of producing a longer piece, perhaps using a different tune file. At this stage the children were becoming familiar with the program, and the majority now understood how to:

    select and place the pictures where they wanted them
    alter the placing of pictures if they needed
    change the speed of their music
    save their piece onto the disc
    fetch their piece back from the disc
    print out a copy of their piece

Given this familiarity I decided the children were ready for the slightly more complicated task of writing some words to their pieces. To introduce this we came together as a class to write some words to a few of the basic pictures from the Compose 1 tune file. The children were encouraged to listen carefully to the rhythm of each picture so that the words would fit. After that they went back into their groups to write some-thing of their own. The children surprised me in two ways at this point. Firstly, the way in which they used the facilities the program offered, such as slowing the music down and freezing individual pictures, to help them in their task, and secondly the apparent ease with which many of them produced very good words. Writing words to music is normally quite difficult unless you know the music very well, but the COMPOSE Program makes it into an interesting and enjoyable task.

At this point we branched off slightly from the more musical aspects of COMPOSE to use the facilities it offers for produc-

Compose Help

Some useful keys:

L   to listen to individual pictures
         and RETURN to select pictures
P   to play your tune
S   to save your tune
F   to fetch a tune from disc
D   to dump a screen to the printer
C   to clear the screen and start again
K   to select continuous play
SPACE BAR to stop the tune when it is playing
1...9   to change the speed of your tune
COPY   to freeze the tune while it is playing
£   to turn the computer volume down
DELETE   to delete a picture
COPY   to add a picture in the middle of a tune
H   for more help

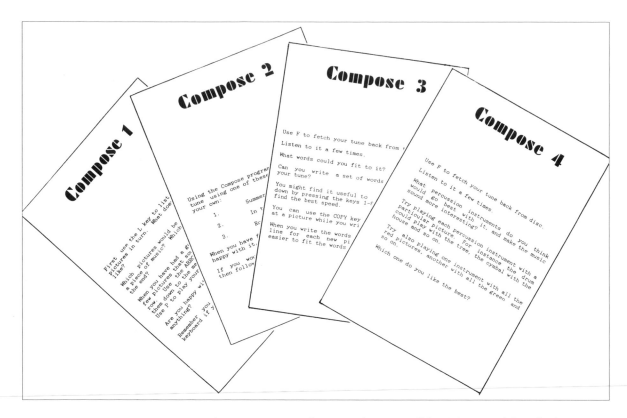

ing your own pictures. As part of the Maps and Symbols project the children had been looking at weather and weather symbols. We therefore decided to make up a set of weather pictures to go with a tune file. Having decided as a class the sort of symbols that would be suitable, and having shown the children the way to construct and edit their own pictures, they set to work in their groups. As the picture editor uses a 24 by 24 grid for its pictures, the children initially used squared paper to try out their designs. It is possible to use or edit any of the pictures already in COMPOSE, or to create entirely new ones. (The method of entering the pictures onto the computer is fairly straightforward and is well explained in the instruction book.)

Tune file devised by children

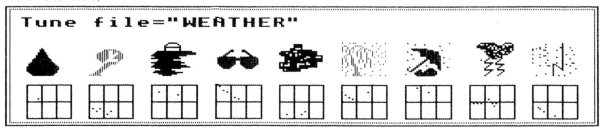

The children produced some exciting pictures and then went onto the next stage of choosing some tunes to go with them. COMPOSE allows you to pick up or edit any tune from other tune files to use in your own file, or to create new ones. However, creating new tunes is a rather more difficult task than producing new pictures, so we opted for a set of existing tune files. The children enjoyed the opportunity to compose with their own pictures, and were particularly keen to find out what 'their' musical phrase sounded like.

Using the editor in this way is of course a way in which COMPOSE can be tailored to fit particular themes or projects.

Particularly in the early stages of its use, COMPOSE caused a great deal of interest in the semi-open-plan area where the computer and keyboard were positioned. However other children in the vicinity on the whole enjoy the background music, and the sounds are generally pleasing!

It is almost immediately obvious when using COMPOSE that the children enjoy using the program. They quickly learn to find their way around the keys, and so the software presents little barrier to their creativity. They start to recognize and remember the individual pictures and their associated phrases straight away, and often sing them aloud as they work around the computer. Many children like to investigate the other facilities the program has to offer, particularly the different tune files. (The Chinese and Eygptian ones always seem to be very popular.) Some also like to experiment with different-sized screens; however, as many of them like to fill all the available space, and the largest screen can have up to eighty phrases, the resulting compositions can be rather lengthy!

Children always relish an opportunity to have a print-out of what they have been doing, and in our school this is certainly a much-used feature. For a group to have a copy each, photo-copying a single print-out is more practical than waiting for a number to be printed. The print-outs make a pleasant display and promote discussion amongst the children. One suggestion that I haven't yet tried is writing a story using the pictures from the printout as a stimulus. This may offer opportunities for integrating the COMPOSE work still further.

There is a wide range of different styles available from the tune files on the normal disc, and using some of them the children can produce compositions in styles they might not otherwise come across. In addition other tune files are available separately, offering not only a wider range of styles, but also a different way of using COMPOSE. Instead of using totally new

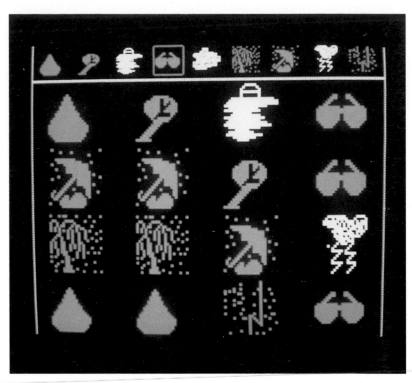

The 'Rainy Day' tune on screen

tunes in the files, well-known tunes split into sections are included for the children to 'un-jumble'. A Special Needs version is also available, and in Chapter 10 Chris Hopkins discusses her Concept Keyboard adaptation for use by sight-impaired children.

Conclusion

COMPOSE offers the child a friendly environment to learn in, one where there are no right or wrong answers — a place to try out ideas, then change them if need be, an open-ended approach which is a feature of many successful programs. Musically, what makes the program so good is that the children are having to make compositional decisions based on what they are hearing. They have to decide which pictures make good beginnings, which make good ends, and so on. This constant choice of a range of possibilities is the very essence of musical composition. However, because in COMPOSE the choices are not too endless (only nine possible melodic cells), and because the graphics make identification and selection of phrases easy, the program is a superb way of introducing and developing composition with children, as well as a good introduction to computer control of music.

Additional Programs for Primary Music

Andy Pierson has produced a number of programs offering many opportunities for creativity in classroom music, some of which are mentioned briefly below. He is very active writing and carrying out extensive classroom trials on new software, and is currently involved in a new version of COMPOSE with multiple parts. The new Acorn Archimedes computer with its higher-quality stereo sound capabilities offers much greater versatility and, provided the Archimedes appears in sufficient numbers in schools, should produce some interesting new software. A version of COMPOSE is already in existence for the Archimedes computer.

COMPOSING AND EXPERIMENTING WITH MUSIC is a set of programs published by Longmans which includes several programs of interest to the Primary teacher, namely COMBINE, ZIG and HIGHLIGHT. All the programs offer MIDI facilities, in some cases quite comprehensive.

RHYTHM MAKER is a program that allows you to compose using drum-type sounds created by the computer itself, and then combine these into longer pieces. It also has facilities for controlling the drum sounds on external devices, such as keyboards, via MIDI.

COMPOSE 2 — at the time of writing this is only at the ideas stage, but it is an exciting development of the original COMPOSE, allowing the use of up to three parts simultaneously. When it appears it will certainly be a program to try out.

In the meantime, the first version of COMPOSE, using only the basic BBC computer, can stimulate and enhance musical activities for children and teachers who have little or no traditional music expertise. Those teachers who understandably find it difficult to include music in their day-to-day activities are likely to find they can offer a broader curriculum to their pupils without automatically seeking the help of a musician.

Programs Mentioned

Compose
Compose 2
Composing and Experimenting with Music (Combine, Zig and
    Highlight)
Rhythm Maker

12 Creative Activities: Art and Design

Tim Royle

The use of computers in education has caused major changes in the past few years, not least of which have been those involving manipulation of graphic images. The implications for developments in visual education are obvious and although there is a great deal of potential yet to be realized, much good work has been achieved.

The major problem resulting from the rapid pace of change is ensuring that sufficient consideration is given to the relevance and value of available software in terms of educational purposes, and the ways and means of underpinning use of the new technology with appropriate teaching and learning strategies.

The majority of primary school teachers have little time to spend finding and evaluating software, let alone relating that which is available to classroom practice and curriculum development. Faced with a bewildering and ever increasing range of programmes, many are inhibited, disarmed and unsure of how they can make good use of the new technology in the curriculum.

This chapter sets out to identify ways in which the use of computers in art and design can enrich the educational diet of primary school pupils, and give examples of both discrete and collaborative projects which reflect current practice.

Most programs available for the BBC microcomputer are user-friendly and after an initial period of time spent on familiarization they can be brought into use in the classroom. The preference will be for programs that offer sufficient flexibility and versatility to make a broad contribution to learning.

Computer graphics are in widespread use by professional artists and designers and evidence of this can be seen daily on our television screens, but this new medium is not a substitute for existing art and design materials.

Good practice in art and design education has always involved the provision of an exciting range of visual and personal stimuli to motivate and support pupils in their work, and discussion about such resources is a basic strategy used by good class teachers. This is just as relevant in relation to the new technology. For computers in art and design to make an effective contribution to learning, their use must be firmly embedded in the creative process rather than simply as an interesting diversion, or a short cut to a finished product.

Pupils learn more quickly about operating an art and design computer program if they explore its features and elements in small groups rather than individually. In this respect, observation and discussion by members of the group is an important

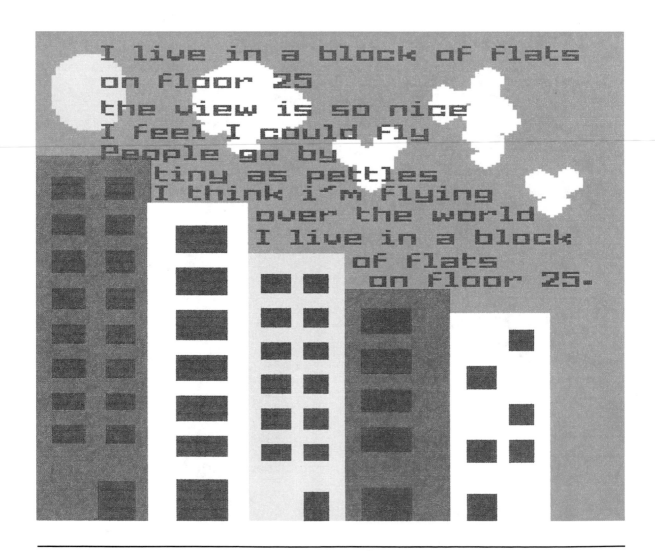

system in developing the individual's self-confidence. For pupils to acquire knowledge of the basic technical aspects of using art and design software, it will help enormously if in the first instance observation and discussion have played a major part in their experience.

The Value of Computers in Art and Design

In justifying the use of computers in creative activities, the following points may prove helpful.

The computer and its attendant software represent an additional medium, increasing the range and breadth of art and design resources. In an increasingly computer-literate society this significant contemporary tool offers a foundation for access to future creative technology.

Detailed technical knowledge of computers is not a prerequisite. Children can achieve exciting results using just a small proportion of the available facilities, developing their skills and knowledge gradually and at their own pace. It is appropriate for use by all ages and abilities, and the professional quality of the work produced can be a strong motivating influence on children.

Where children encounter problems with coordination and manipulative skills using conventional materials, the computer provides them with the opportunity to achieve a degree of precision that would otherwise not have been possible. The demotivating influence in such situations is lessened.

A feature of most of the available software is that it is not prescriptive, but offers open-ended opportunities to develop ideas related to a whole range of learning situations across the curriculum.

The labour-saving nature of computers has major implications for the nature of the learning process. Because of the speed at which changes can be made to an image, children have more time to become involved in analyzing aspects of their work — such as colour and shape relationships, composition, texture and scale. Children working in groups creating images are more inclined to enter into discussion about work in progress and as the work is seen 'on screen' simultaneously by all children in the group, critical activities can develop readily. Through group work children begin to share responsibility for their own learning.

The storage facility enables uninhibited development of work because of the security of always being able to retrieve previous images, including the original, from the disc. This can be invaluable in recording the development process. Each stage of a piece of work can be retrieved, printed off and displayed as and when required. The end of a session does not have to mean the end of the work. Children can return to their work at a later date and carry on where they left off. This is important in that shared access to a computer within a group is the only realistic way of ensuring the opportunity to use the computer is afforded to all children.

A major feature is the scope for experimental and investigative work. Due to the labour-saving nature of the technology, alternatives can be tried, pictorial and letter images can be combined and thinking and planning skills can be encouraged, leading to the development of graphic awareness.

Getting Started

In Berkshire schools a number of programs have been tried and tested, and some have proved to be more versatile than others. The popular choice is IMAGE which stands for Image Maker for Artistic and Graphic Experimentation. This program is published by the Cambridge University Press, and is particularly significant in that very sophisticated results can be achieved by users with little or no previous experience of computers, and a wide range of printers and input devices can be accommodated. Importantly, Fred Daly, who designed the program, established a working group of teachers and art educators to help and advise throughout the development process. This ensured that needs as perceived by those involved in classroom practice were met as far as possible.

In using a computer graphics package as a medium for art and design it is essential that a balance is achieved between power, flexibility and ease of use. This is certainly the case with IMAGE, which is suitable for all ages and abilities.

Before discussing the possible applications of computer-related art and design, it is important to outline the main features and the range of equipment that can be used in conjunction with it.

In addition to the computer, monitor and single or dual disc drive, a colour printer and a pointing device are needed.

Although a black and white printer can produce interesting results based on levels of grey, a colour printer is essential to make full use of the technology. A range of pointing devices can be used including a joystick, mouse, graphpad and Concept Keyboard.

The pointing device enables the user to move the cursor around the screen either selecting options from pull-out menus and colours from the basic palette of eight, or building up lines, shapes, patterns and text.

A range of options are available for use, and can be combined in the production process. Lines can be drawn in various thickness, geometric shapes can be constructed of any size in both solid and line form. Colour mixing and manipulation enable the basic palette to be extended or changed round and a wide range of textures and patterns can be created, used and kept within the program's store.

Sections of an image can be selected and scaled up or down, distorted, rotated, reflected and repeated. Areas of the screen can be isolated and the remainder wiped away.

At any point during the development of an image, it can be saved on disc for future reference and use, thereby allowing the user to take risks and experiment without losing valuable work.

The text facility offers two font styles and letters and words of any size can be constructed and positioned on screen.

For those with access to a video camera, an additional equipment item well worth acquiring is a digitizer. Live pictures can be captured and manipulated with the program features. This extends the potential of the system, and offers scope for the selection of ready-made images and movement to be recorded and analyzed, any aspect of which can be incorporated into pupils' work.

Primary schools with access to Archimedes or Nimbus machines, which have far greater power, will have the benefit of a wider range of program features. A dramatic increase in the number of colours available and the speed of response makes them highly desirable, but the general operating principles are the same.

Project Examples

The following open-ended projects are presented to afford primary school teachers examples of how the use of computers in art and design can be integrated into the general learning experience.

They are not meant to be prescriptive but to offer possible frameworks on which to build relative to particular needs and abilities. All the examples have collaborative potential and can be expanded upon as necessary.

Each example includes reference to secondary source material which can enrich and enhance the range of projects. Access to specific artists' work can be gained from a variety of sources including books, prints, slides and postcards.

The first three examples are concerned with design-orientated activities and the remainder offer scope for more expressive work.

Significantly, all are concerned with Recording, Analyzing, Communicating and Expressing, and encourage the development of visual literacy through investigative work.

It is left to the individual to decide how best to relate these suggestions to their own practice. The emphasis is placed on process rather than product, the acquisition of observational, critical and making skills and their appropriate application.

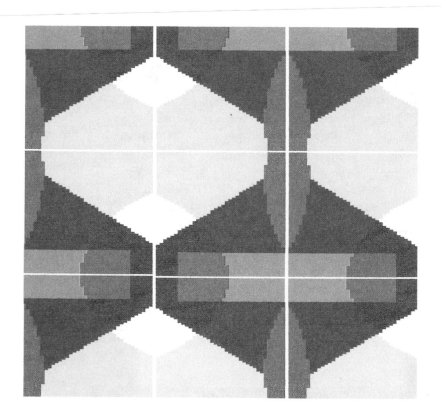

Project One: Pattern

Pattern making, normally a slow, repetitive and difficult precision skill, can be made much more exciting given the immediacy of computer response. What would have taken a considerable amount of time with paper and pencil can be achieved much more quickly on a computer. Consequently children can focus on analysis and selection, moving the emphasis to the creative process.

Aim

To develop an understanding of pattern construction and its potential for creating optical effects and illusions.

Project Outline

Look at and discuss examples of pattern. Note the relationships between shapes and colours, and the different effects degrees of detail can create.

Using three or four shapes, plan a simple repeating sequence on paper. Try several alternatives. Avoid using too many colours.

On the computer, copy and develop your patterns. Experiment with different colours and shape sizes

Note how your pattern appears to change depending on the colours selected.

Resources/Reference

Tesselations
Islamic patterns
Textile designs
Natural patterns

ARTISTS
Bridget Riley
Vaserely

Project Two: Personal Logo

Aim

To develop an understanding of compositional skills, and an awareness of how information can be condensed to form a symbolic image.

Project Outline

From magazines and other sources, collect as many different examples of logos as possible. Discuss how words and images can be combined.

Using your own name or initials, develop ideas on paper exploring the possibilities of fitting them into or around geometric shapes. Divide up a range of geometric shapes into the number of spaces appropriate for your name or initials, e.g. segments of a circle, diagonals of squares and rectangles.

On the computer, develop your ideas incorporating colour. Try positive and negative effects, light letters on a dark background and dark letters on a light background. Experiment with different sizes of letters and shapes.

Consider how your ideas can be developed through collage, i.e. cutting letters and backgrounds out of magazines etc.

Make a list of things that you like or are important to you, e.g. your favourite colour, sport, food, etc. On paper develop a simple image from your list, and consider how you could combine it with your name and initials.

Develop your ideas on the computer.

Project Three: Project Book Title Page

Aim

To develop awareness of the importance of presentation, to increase motivation and develop pride in work.

Project Outline

Collect together a wide range of examples of book covers, posters, border designs and patterns. Discuss how letter size variation can give emphasis to certain words, and how colour and shape can be used to draw attention to specific details.

In relation to a piece of your own work, consider alternative layout styles. Bear in mind the importance of economic and careful selection of words and images. Avoid unnecessary complication and clutter. Develop ideas on paper. Transfer one of them onto the computer screen and experiment with scale, centring, reflection, mirror imaging and colour.

Experiment with alternative background colours or patterns.

Resources/Reference

Book covers
Posters
Illuminated manuscripts
Islamic patterns

ARTISTS
William Morris
Aubrey Beardsley

Project Four: Colour Mixing

One of the most important elements of any programme of study involving colour is to enable children to encounter as rich and varied a range of materials and processes as possible. Investigative work, with opportunities for comparing and contrasting the visual effects created by different media, has far more relevance than simple and traditional colour mixing exercises.

Aim

To enable pupils to develop an awareness of the effects different colours can create, and confidence in mixing and applying colour.

Project Outline

Through class discussion explore the properties of colour and how colours symbolize different things, e.g. Blue — cold, sad, etc., Red — hot, danger, etc.

Using a card viewfinder and coloured acetates, observe the effects created by viewing the same image through a range of colours.

Identify three kinds of red, yellow and blue either directly observed from objects in the classroom or from secondary source material. Using paint, try to match through careful mixing. Experiment with ways of applying colour using combinations of dabs or blending.

On the computer, repeat the exercise using the colour mixing facility, overlapping colours and direct markmaking. Compare the effects with those made on paper.

Colours often have specific names, e.g. grass green, ruby red, primrose yellow, sky blue etc. Create names that you feel describe the colours you have made.

Look at how artists have used a variety of ways to apply colour. What effects were they trying to achieve?

From imagination, make a picture that is predominantly one colour and expresses the feelings and mood associated with it.

Resources/Reference

Paint
Coloured acetates
Card viewfinders

ARTISTS
Seurat
Lichtenstein
Albers
Derain
Monet
Van Gogh

Project Five: Geometric Shape Exercise

Aim

To develop spacial awareness in relation to overlapping shapes.

Project Outline

Make a list of geometric shapes and draw an example next to each one.

Select three, and make large templates out of card. Use the templates to draw round, and build up a composition by overlapping them. Notice the new shapes created by overlapping. See how many new shapes you can create in this way.

Using the shape facility on the computer, repeat the exercise, adding shapes and colours as necessary. Experiment with scale and overlapping techniques. Try using the minimum number of colours so that no two adjacent areas are the same.

Develop a picture based on your experiments. Avoid over-complication.

Project Six: Faces

Aim

To record from observation in written and drawn form and to develop an imaginative response.

Project Outline

Look at examples of faces in books, magazines and artists' work. Discuss the variety of features and characteristics they depict.

Make a list of the characteristics. Add to each one its opposite, e.g. Young — Old, Kind — Mean, Happy — Sad, etc.

Select sufficient of these to make a drawing of a face based on them. Working in pairs, take turns to model for your partner.

Copy your drawing onto the computer screen, and store your character on disc.

Explore the possibility of changing some of the characteristics to produce an imaginary creature, e.g. Monster, Alien.

Using stage make-up try to recreate the creature on your face. Take a photograph.

Resources/Reference

African masks
Japanese prints
Comic strips
Cartoons
Caricatures

ARTISTS
Van Gogh
Picasso
Lichtenstein
Wyndham Lewis
Ralph Steadman

Project Seven: Composition

Aim

To enable pupils to explore simple principles of composition, and to organize images with confidence.

Project Outline

Discuss the meaning of composition and the elements involved:

1. Arrangement and selection of the content of a picture.
2. Contrast — shapes, textures and colours.
3. Perspective — explain basic principles, e.g. colour recession, things appearing to be smaller in the distance, eye level, etc.

Look at examples of interesting composition. Choose a spot in the school grounds from where it is possible to select a view which includes part of the building, something in the foreground and something in the distance. Make at least one objective drawing of this using coloured pencils, pastels or chalks. Ensure that different marks are made to indicate textures.

On the computer, experiment with different ways of making marks, using lines, dots, shapes and flat areas. Relate your experiments to the picture you have drawn.

Resources/Reference

ARTISTS
Hockney
Lowry
Cézanne

Program Mentioned

Image

The Education Reform Act 1988 underlines the importance of design and technological activity across the curriculum. Art and Design has an important contribution to make to this area of experience, and the use of IT systems to form and manipulate graphic images has specific relevance.

Currently much of the work developing in schools offers a significant and dynamic enhancement to learning. In a world where over 80 per cent of knowledge is gained visually, it is particularly important that the potential of computers in art and design is fully utilized and maximum advantage is taken of the exciting possibilities that future developments hold.

In the period of time in which this book was compiled, further developments have brought higher quality and greater versatility. The introduction of scanners and digitizers, coupled with significant software improvements, have enabled complete flexibility in capturing and generating images. Combined with text facilities, the power to express and communicate imagination, ideas and feelings in a professional form surely places this area of experience at the forefront of the technological revolution.

13   Developing a
School Policy

Denby Richards

Although it is now widely accepted that computers are an integral part of the learning process in schools this, unlike most other aspects of education, is a fairly recent phenomenon and lacks an historical base. In addition, the increasing sophistication of all aspects of Information Technology means that we are in increasing danger of being seduced by bright images and complex calculations. It is, therefore, vitally important that the use of computers is placed within a sound educational framework. The following is an account of the computer policy of one school and the factors that influenced its development. Though this policy is the result of a number of years' experience it may prove to be a useful guide for those undergoing or about to undergo the same process. Though many of the decisions arose from particular needs and circumstances, the underlying philosophy should be appropriate to many situations.

What Aims do we have for Computer Use?

The school policy for computer use is based around two fundamental aims. Firstly, that computers should be viewed as a tool that children and staff should feel able to use comfortably and profitably. Secondly, the use of computers should be integral to and supportive of the curriculum offered to the children. These decisions, though reached some time ago and regularly reviewed, are still felt to be appropriate. Any further decisions we have made or will make about the use of computers must satisfy these two criteria. The following sections deal with our approach to the organization and management of the computer, a process needing periodic review, an important component of any policy. The structure we have devised is the result of seven years of computer use and no doubt should and will be influenced by advances as immediate as those happening tomorrow. A note of caution, however, must be sounded: the adoption of hardware and software and new ways of using the computer must arise from an identified need or use within the curriculum. That is not to say, however, that we should not always be alert to the possibility of offering children new experiences opened up by the rapidity of technological advance.

The Child, the Curriculum and the Computer

Because we believe it is important that computer use should be supportive of the curriculum offered to the children this must be our starting-point in deciding its use. We see our curriculum as having two broad aims: (i) to develop skills and (ii) to offer

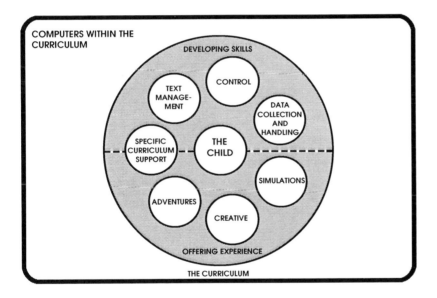

experience, the two being interlinked within an integrated approach. It is important, therefore, that our computer use mirrors these aims. For this reason we have not adopted a narrow curriculum-specific approach but we have, as can be seen from the diagram above, defined seven general areas of support that the computer can offer. Our aim is that children should have the opportunity to use computers in these areas at a level appropriate to their development. Again it should be noted that this is our present model and that whilst some areas are well established others are for us innovatory. We therefore need to realize that this structure may change.

The Organization

The Role of the Coordinator

A crucial factor in our development of computer use was the recognition that it was necessary for somebody to act as a coordinator with a brief similar to that of our established curriculum coordinators. The coordinator is required:

— to have an overview of present use throughout the school and also its continuing development specifically in relation to the School Development Plan
— to keep up to date with current aspects of computer use by attending courses and subscribing to relevant publications
— to cast a critical eye over present use and proposed purchases
— to be responsible for the organization and management of hardware and software, its repair and maintenance
— to draw up, in consultation with colleagues, a bid for hardware and software purchase as part of annual budget discussions.

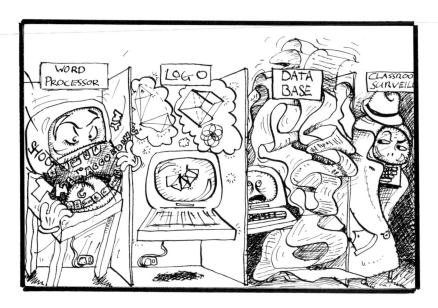

Dedicated computers?

The most important element of the post, however, relates to in-service work. Not only should the coordinator act as a resource and be able to point colleagues in the direction of relevant county courses and other sources of external input but he or she should also organize in-school activities. Without an established pattern of in-school support and backup there is little hope of establishing consistent good practice. One approach we have found productive is the concentration for a predetermined period on a single aspect of computer use. In order to establish the computer as a writing tool the coordinator ran a series of workshops to introduce the two word-processing programs we had decided to use. Time was spent discussing the differing contexts within which children write and how the computer could enhance these. Opportunities were provided for hands-on experience backed up by duplicated notes detailing main points and suggestions for use. The staff then followed these sessions up by using the programs in their own classrooms. This led to a unanimous decision to equip all our computers with printers as the next hardware policy.

Organizing the Hardware

Not only is it important to have a structure for using present equipment effectively but it is also important to have a clear plan of future requirements and the attendant resource implications. The school, a 5 to 12 combined school, is organized in three phases, each having a complete system, computer, disc drive and printer attached to it. Each system is housed on a purpose-built trolley that can be wheeled into a secure store at the end of the day. Its use is timetabled amongst the three classes by the Phase Coordinator. Whilst the pattern of use is fairly flexible the computer in most cases will spend a week with each class. The fourth system at present enjoys a peripatetic role, spending half a term with each phase, although it is also available should a class or phase need it full-time for a mutually agreed period to pursue a particular task. In addition the Lower Phase system has a Concept Keyboard attached to it whilst other peripherals, buggy, turtle and mouse are kept centrally for use as needed. The present plan for future purchases envisages each classroom with its own system. Beyond that we would like to see the day when a classroom contains a number of machines, some permanently dedicated to specific tasks like word-processing or Logo.

Organizing the Software

Initially each computer was supplied with a disc box containing copies of all the programs that were currently in use. This

SOFTWARE TO SUPPORT AREAS OF COMPUTER USE WITHIN THE CURRICULUM

	TEXT MANAGEMENT	CURRICULUM SUPPORT	DATA HANDLING	CREATIVE	ADVENTURES	SIMULATIONS	CONTROL
FILES	WRITING (2)	LANGUAGE (2) MATHS (3) *	DATABASE (2) SENSORS	CREATIVE	ADVENTURES (2) *	TOPIC (2) *	TURTLE GRAPHICS BBC BUGGY WALK
1st PHASE	PROMPT WRITER (CONCEPT KEYBOARD) PENDOWN FRONT PAGE EXTRA	POD MOVING IN GUSINTER WORDPLAY	OURSELVES (PRESENT FILES)	COMPOSE SIGNWRITER	LOST FROG PUFF	JUMBO FIREWORK SAFETY	WALK DELTA (VALIANT TURTLE) BUGGY
2nd PHASE	NEWS BULLETIN	COLONY TRAY	OURSELVES (OWN FILES) TEMPERATURE AND LIGHT SENSOR	IMAGE (MOUSE)	DRAGON WORLD DINOSAUR DISCOVERY	NORMAN ENGLAND LOCKS POND DIPPING	
3rd PHASE			GRASS	FONT EDITOR	WIZARDS REVENGE	MARY ROSE EXTRA	

* Examples of programs available in these areas. They should not be treated as prescriptive.
Software should be chosen to suit the needs of the child or to initiate or extend the topic chosen.

system, however, soon became unwieldy as not only the number but type and scope of programs increased, many requiring extensive use of associated materials. It was then decided to make up ring binders containing suites of similar programs each fitting into one of the seven broad areas of use agreed upon. One danger when putting together a software catalogue is the 'squirrel effect', but it is important to bear in mind that quality not quantity must be the overriding factor. If the criteria used are that programs should be educationally sound and also fulfil a particular need then there is no reason why all the staff should not feel able to help select suitable software. Above all one should not be afraid to jettison poor programs even if they were given free by an eager parent. At present we find that just two word-processing packages and two database programs are adequate for all the work the children do in these areas. Within each ring binder the discs are kept in plastic wallets whilst associated materials are punched for ease of removal and use. As we have two staffrooms a copy of each file is kept in each room and are taken out by staff as and when needed. As one room serves the lower part of the school the files in some cases are not identical; for example the Adventure files contain a slightly different but overlapping range of programs. Each member of staff is furnished with a copy of the software plan to use in conjunction with curriculum documents when planning work, and suggestions are made as to when a piece of software could be introduced and in which context. This is of course not prescriptive and individual teachers are able to seek further guidance from the coordinator. We have also found it useful not only to back up software but also associated materials where possible. These are housed for safe keeping in a locked cabinet and are only used for making copies. In addition a supply of blank formatted discs is kept available for saving text and data files.

Meeting the Challenge

There can be no ideal structure for using computers in schools. Our present model is the result of many factors, not least the commitment of staff to the importance of the computer as a tool for learning. What is important is that the school has a clear rationale based upon the perceived needs of the children and the resources available. This will then in turn form a secure basis for meeting the continuing challenge that computers and Information Technology will place before children and teachers.

Discussion Points

Is there a clear rationale behind the use of computers?
Is it relevant to the curriculum offered to the children?
Is it necessary to develop a coordinators role?
If so what are the important components of that role?
How can the present resources be used effectively for all the children?
Is there a systematic plan for future hardware and software purchase and development?
Is there in-service support available and is it being used?
Would it be useful to concentrate on a particular area of use as a means of consolidating practice?
Are the staff developing the ability to judge new software critically?

14 Technical Tips

Howard Gillings and David Griffiths

This section of the book is aimed at those people who are feeling happy about using computers in the classroom but feel the need for a little more technical knowledge to help them organize the computer's use more effectively in their classroom or within their school. A little technical knowledge can help you overcome those irritating problems that the 'expert' fixes with a flick of the finger and a knowing smile.

The BBC Microcomputer System

The BBC Microcomputer System comes in three essential parts — the computer and keyboard, the monitor and the disc drive. After you receive a new system or move your system around it will be necessary to put it together carefully so that it works correctly.

Once you have positioned the items of equipment approximately where you want them, first thread the ribbon cable from the disc drive under the computer and plug it in under the front of the computer into the socket labelled 'disc drive'. Ensure the plug is inserted the right way round by matching the protruding lug on the plug to the gap in the socket. When you press the plug fully into the socket the clips on the socket will close and grip the plug. If the disc drive does not have a mains power lead with an ordinary 13 amp plug on it, it will have a special power cable which plugs in under the computer in the socket labelled 'auxiliary power output'. Care should be taken in inserting and removing this lead.

The lead which connects the monitor to the computer has an identical six-pin DIN plug on each end. When inserting the

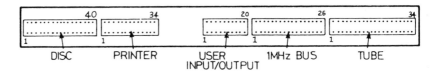

Position of sockets underneath the computer

plugs ensure that the plug is the right way round with the notch in the plug correctly aligned.

Once the items of hardware are connected together the mains plugs can be plugged in and switched on. When switching the system on it is best to switch the computer on last. Should any peripherals fail to work correctly check that:

they are plugged into their power supply and switched on

they are connected to the computer correctly

all leads are firmly in place and undamaged

the peripheral is ready for use

you have used the correct commands within the program

If all this fails try using the suspect equipment on a different computer system which you know is working properly.

DO NOT ATTEMPT TO REMOVE THE COVERS FROM EQUIPMENT TO CHECK THE INNER WORKINGS

The BBC Master Computer

The BBC Master 128 Computer is different from the original BBC 'B' in a number of ways. One of the ways which is of immediate concern when you first receive the computer is the availability of a choice of disc filing systems. These filing systems, the 1770 DFS and the ADFS (Advanced Disc Filing System) use a different disc format which prevents the interchange of discs between filing systems. When the computer is delivered it is most likely to be set up to use the ADFS as this is the format used on the Welcome Disc supplied with the computer. The discs used in school are usually in DFS format and will not, therefore, work. In order to overcome this problem the computer needs to be re-configured.

To select the standard DFS type

⋆CONFIGURE FILE9 〈RETURN〉
then press **CTRL** and tap **BREAK.**

To select the ADFS type

⋆CONFIGURE FILE13 〈RETURN〉
then press **CTRL** and tap **BREAK.**

Once the machine is configured in the way you require it will remain in this state whenever you switch on. You do not have to go through the re-configuring process each time you use the computer.

The Monitor

The monitors used with the BBC Computer are normally reliable. If there is no picture on the screen then first of all check that the brilliance control is set correctly, then check the monitor and the computer are switched on and the leads are plugged in and undamaged. If these remedies fail the equipment should be checked.

Disc Drives and Discs

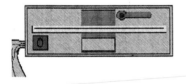

A single disc drive

You can purchase a variety of different types of disc drive to plug into your BBC Computer. The most common is the single disc drive.

Although many of the older disc drives were capable of using only one side of the disc formatted with forty tracks (see below) many of the modern drives can use both sides of the disc and can be switched between forty and eighty tracks. It is possible to purchase a dual disc drive which allows two discs to be inserted simultaneously. This type of drive is particularly useful for

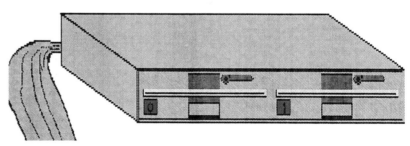

A dual disc drive

copying files from one disc to another and for some of the more advanced programs which require the use of more than one disc.

How to Find out what is on a Disc

Although most commercial discs are carefully labelled there will eventually be a time when you need to see which files or programs are on a disc you have prepared.

This information is held in the disc catalogue and can be seen by typing

⋆CAT ⟨RETURN⟩

or its abbreviation

⋆.⟨RETURN⟩

The screen display will look something like this:

DISC-TITLE (13)
Drive 0	**Option 0 (OFF)**
Dir. :0.$	**Lib. :0.$**
DRAGONS	**DRAINS**
STORY	**ENGINE**
W.DREAMS	**W.DISCS**
W.TRAINS	

This shows that the disc is titled 'DISC-TITLE' and has seven files or programs saved on it. Each program name can have up to seven letters and can be preceded by a single letter and full stop to give the program a directory name. This name is the one which the computer uses to identify the program or file and need not bear any relation to the contents of the file — although it helps if you use reasonably meaningful names!

If you have more than one drive then each drive can be catalogued by typing the drive number after ⋆CAT, e.g.

⋆CAT 1 ⟨RETURN⟩

will give a catalogue of the disc in drive 1. If you catalogue a disc and the computer fails to find the catalogue then it is likely that the disc has not been formatted. Blank discs are not prepared in any way for holding programs or any other data. The disc has to be formatted before use.

Formatting a Disc

When you purchase a new disc it will be totally blank. Discs are provided in this state as different computers require different formats on the disc for them to work. The discs that each computer system uses must be formatted to match the disc drive and the computer. This is done using a program specially written for the purpose which is provided with the computer or the disc drive. In the case of the ordinary BBC micro the formatting program is provided with the disc drive when you purchase it while with the BBC B + and the BBC Master 128 the formatting program is part of the computer's Disc Filing System.

When the computer formats a disc it places an electronic pattern on the disc which consists of a series of concentric rings called tracks each split into sectors. There can be forty or eighty tracks each with ten sectors. The information stored on the disc is stored on these sectors.

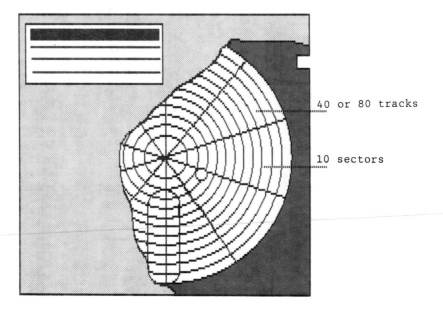

40 or 80 tracks

10 sectors

Cut away diagram of a floppy disc

If you are formatting a disc you should insert the disc and then follow the instructions provided with it. This will generally mean either 'booting' the disc or typing ∗FORM and pressing RETURN. If you are using a B + or a Master simply type ∗FORM 40 ⟨RETURN⟩ for a forty-track drive or ∗FORM 80 ⟨RETURN⟩ for an eighty-track drive. In all cases you should then insert a blank disc in the disc drive and follow the prompt on the screen which asks which drive. Normally, if you have a single disc drive, this will be drive 0. You should take particular care if you are reformatting a disc you have already been using or if you are unsure if the disc is formatted or not, as formatting completely removes all existing information from the disc!

Most commercially available educational programs are available on formatted discs that can be started automatically by holding down the SHIFT key and tapping the BREAK key or, to use the jargon, 'booting' the disc. This will either give a menu of all the programs on the disc and allow you to select the one you require by pressing a letter or a number or, if there is only one program on the disc, will run the program immediately.

The easiest way to see if a disc will work in this way is to try it! It is however very easy to see whether the disc is set up to auto-boot or not simply by examining the disc catalogue. On the catalogue there should be a file called !BOOT and at the top right the OPTION should be set at 1, 2 or 3. If either of these cases is not true then the disc will not auto-boot. A typical disc catalogue, where the disc is set up to auto-boot, looks like this

DISC TITLE (13)
Drive 0   **Option 3 (EXEC)**
Dir. :0.$**   **Lib. :0.$
!BOOT   **DRAGONS**
DRAINS   **STORY**
W.DREAMS   **W.DISCS**
W.TRAINS

If these two items are not present on the disc, then you will need to set the disc up as follows.

The !BOOT File

This is a number of instructions that are acted on when the disc is auto-booted. The most common !BOOT file has only one instruction which tells the computer to CHAIN another program — often a menu program which allows you to CHAIN any of the programs on the disc. In order to construct a !BOOT file proceed as follows:

Place the disc in the disc drive, first ensuring there is not a !BOOT file present and type

★BUILD !BOOT ⟨RETURN⟩

The disc drive will whirr and the screen will then show a number 1 or 001.

Type in the instructions you need following each one by pressing RETURN, e.g.

001 CHAIN "MENU"
002

When you have finished typing your instructions press ESCAPE. The disc drive will whirr again.

If you now catalogue the disc you will see that there is now a !BOOT file saved on the disc.

The Option

It is now necessary to set the loading OPTION to either 1, 2 or 3. Normally OPTION 3 — execute the !BOOT file — is used.
To set this option type

★OPT 4,3 ⟨RETURN⟩

The·disc drive will whirr. Cataloguing the disc will now show at the top right Option 3 (EXEC).

The disc is now ready for auto-booting. Try holding down SHIFT and tapping BREAK to see if it works.

Copying Discs

It is always advisable when you purchase a disc or save some important files to make a copy of the disc in case the disc fails to work or suffers from an accident which makes it unusable.

You should not copy discs for any other purpose or you will be infringing copyright. Many commercially produced discs are protected from copying to prevent copyright abuse. If these discs fail to work then they should be returned to the supplier. When you have made a copy of a disc you should keep the original in a safe place and use the copy. It is very important that the disc in common use is not the only copy you have — replacing valuable programs or files can be expensive or time-consuming or both.

How to Copy a Complete Disc

Making a backup copy of a disc is very straightforward. Using a single drive type

★ENABLE ⟨RETURN⟩
★BACKUP 0 0 ⟨RETURN⟩

You will then be prompted to insert the source disc (the one with your programs on it) and press a key. The disc drive will whirr. The next prompt will ask you to insert the destination disc (the one you want the programs copied onto) and press a key. The disc drive will whirr. The process is repeated until the whole disc has been copied.

Take care as this process will erase any programs on the destination disc. The reason for having to type ★ENABLE before ★BACKUP is to warn you of the disaster this command could cause if you are not careful! On the later Disc Filing

Systems there is no need to type ⋆ENABLE, instead you have to confirm the action after entering ⋆BACKUP.

If you are able to use a dual disc drive the process is even simpler. For example, to make a backup from the disc inserted in drive 0 to the disc in drive 1 simply insert the source disc in drive 0 and the destination disc in drive 1, type

⋆ENABLE ⟨RETURN⟩ then **⋆BACKUP 0 1 ⟨RETURN⟩**

and the computer completes the process of copying the disc in a few seconds (you will notice drives 0 and 1 whirring alternately). Make sure you put the source and destination discs in the correct drive or you could wipe your source disc clean!

There will be occasions when you will want to copy a single file or a few files from one disc to another — for instance files of children's work. To do this you should use the command ⋆COPY stating which drive contains the source disc and destination disc and the name of the file to be copied. For example,

⋆COPY 0 0 STORY ⟨RETURN⟩

will copy the file STORY using a single disc drive. In this case you will be asked to put the source disc in the drive and press a key. The disc drive will whirr. You are then prompted to put the destination disc in the drive and press a key. This sequence is repeated until the complete file is copied to the destination disc.

If you have a dual drive copying from disc to disc is much quicker and easier. Once again the source and destination drives must be stated but this time both discs must be inserted in their respective drives. For example,

⋆COPY 0 1 STORY ⟨RETURN⟩

will copy the program STORY from the disc in drive 0 to the disc in drive 1. On pressing RETURN the two drives will whirr alternately until the cursor >__ reappears to signify the process is complete. Copying a program in this way normally takes about five seconds.

How to Prevent your Programs from being Accidentally Erased

When you have set up your discs in the way that you want it is sensible to protect the discs so that they cannot be altered by mistake. This is particularly important for your master discs. The most secure way of protecting your programs once they are on the disc is to stick a tab over the small square notch on the side of the disc. These tabs, called 'write protect tabs', should be provided when you buy the disc. Once you have covered the notch the computer will not allow you to carry out any action on the disc that involves changing what is already on the disc's surface. This is the ideal way of protecting your discs once you have on them the programs you want. Removing the tab will, of course, remove the protection.

A less general way of protecting programs which can protect any or all of the programs on a disc is the use of the command *ACCESS. This command allows you to 'lock' and 'unlock' each program on the disc at will. When a program is locked it can be deleted only by the command *DESTROY, by being the destination disc in *BACKUP or by re-formatting the disc. All the other commands which would erase or change the program are disabled.

*Using *ACCESS*

If you need to protect a file, type

*ACCESS DUMMY L ⟨RETURN⟩

This will lock the program DUMMY thereby protecting it from accidental erasure.

Typing

*ACCESS DUMMY ⟨RETURN⟩

will unlock the program and remove the protection. When a program is locked its entry on the disc's catalogue is followed by an 'L'.

If you are locking or unlocking a number of files dealing with them individually can be a tedious business. It is therefore possible to use the two 'wildcard' characters '#' and '*'. The '#' can be used to represent any single character while the '*' can be used to represent any number of characters. For example, assuming the disc contained the following programs:

DISC1 (13)	
Drive 0	**Option 0 (off)**
Dir. :0.$	**Lib. :0.$**
DRAGONS	**DRAINS**
DUMMY	**STORY**
W.DREAMS	**W.DISCS**
W.TRAINS	

Entering:

★ACCESS D★ L

will lock each file in the current directory (the group of files displayed first in the catalogue without any prefix, in this case the '$' directory), beginning with D. i.e. DRAGON, DRAINS AND DUMMY. The '★' can represent any of the letters following the 'D'.

Entering

★ACCESS #.D★ L

will lock each file in every directory on the disc beginning with D., i.e., DRAGON, DRAINS, DUMMY, W.DREAMS AND W.DISCS.

The '#' can represent the single character of any directory. The '★' has the same effect as in the previous example.

Entering

★ACCESS #.★ L

will lock every unlocked file on the disc, i.e. DRAGON, DRAINS, DUMMY, STORY, W.DREAMS, W.DISCS and W.TRAINS.

The '#' represents the single character of any directory while the '★' represents any combination of letters in any of the filenames. Omitting the 'L' from any of these examples would unlock the corresponding group of programs.

How to Remove an Unwanted File from a Disc

When you are working with files of children's work on a disc there will come a time when a file is no longer needed and it is taking up valuable disc space. It will then be necessary to remove the file from the disc.

There are a number of commands that you can use to remove an unwanted file from a disc. The two most useful are ★DELETE and ★WIPE.

★DELETE allows you to delete a specific file. The file must not have been 'locked' using ★ACCESS. For example,

★DELETE DUMMY

will simply delete the file called DUMMY. When you catalogue the disc you will see that the file is no longer there and there is no gap in the catalogue.

*WIPE is a much more flexible and safer command to use. With *WIPE you can use wildcards in the same way as you can with *ACCESS to specify a number of files as well as just one. Before deleting the file or files the computer lists each file on the screen followed by a colon and awaits confirmation that you really want to wipe off the file. This you do by pressing 'Y'. If you press any other key the computer assumes you mean 'no'. The files must not have been 'locked' using *ACCESS. For example,

*WIPE DUMMY

will prompt with

$.DUMMY:

pressing 'Y' at this point will delete DUMMY: anything else will leave things as they are.

The two wildcard characters, '#' to represent one character and '*' to represent any number of characters, allow the selection of a number of files at the same time; they even allow you to go through all the files on a disc one at a time and either wipe them off or retain them. For example, assume the disc contained the following programs:

DISC1 (13)
Drive 0   **Option 0 (off)**
Dir. :0.$**   **Lib. :0.$
DRAGONS   **DRAINS**
DUMMY   **STORY**
W.DREAMS   **W.DISCS**
W.TRAINS

Entering

WIPE D

will give the option to delete each file in the current directory (the group of files displayed first in the catalogue without any prefix, in this case the $ directory), beginning with D, i.e. DRAGON, DRAINS and DUMMY.

The '*' can represent any of the letters following the 'D'.

Entering

WIPE #.D

will give the option to delete each file in every directory on the disc beginning with D, i.e. DRAGON, DRAINS, DUMMY, W.DREAMS and W.DISCS.

The '#' can represent the single character of any directory. The '*' has the same effect as in the previous example.

Entering

WIPE #.

will give the option to delete every unlocked file on the disc, i.e. DRAGON, DRAINS, DUMMY, STORY, W.DREAMS, W.DISCS and W.TRAINS.

The '#' represents the single character of any directory while the '*' represents any combination of letters in any of the file names.

If you use *WIPE to delete a number of files from a disc you must be very careful not to delete files by mistake as you list through the names on the disc. This is even more important if you have more than one disc in the drives as you could be wiping the wrong disc!

You should always label your discs carefully, keep them in their dust cover in a box and above all keep a backup copy.

Programs on a ROM Chip

While most programs which you will use in school are provided on disc, some of the larger, more sophisticated programs are programmed into a ROM chip (ROM stands for Read Only Memory) which can be plugged into the inside of the computer. Examples of this type of program are PENDOWN, DELTA, EDWORD, WORDWISE and the INTER series of programs. The advantage of this is that the program is available for use as soon as the computer is switched and can be accessed immediately by typing the appropriate command. This command will begin with a '*', e.g. *PD will start up PENDOWN, the children's word-processor.

Inserting the ROM

Inserting the ROM in your computer is a straightforward job, but involves removing the cover from your computer and perhaps removing some of the ROMS already installed.

IF YOU ARE NOT HAPPY ABOUT WORKING ON THE INSIDE OF THE COMPUTER THEN GET THE ROM FITTED BY A DEALER OR OTHER COMPETENT PERSON.

To fit a ROM follow these instructions carefully:

1. Switch off and unplug the computer.
2. Remove the four screws marked 'FIX' — on the BBC B and B + there are two on the bottom and two on the back of the computer while on the Master all four are on the bottom.
3. Remove the top from the computer.
4. On the BBC B only, unscrew the two screws securing the keyboard and gently lift it away to reveal the sockets under its right-hand end. There is no need to unplug the ribbon cable on the back of the keyboard.
5. Check the sockets that are available for the ROMS. As you lift out the keyboard you will see a row of five sockets, two or three of which may be empty. It is important to realize that the order in which the ROMS are placed in the machine can affect the way the computer behaves — especially on the BBC B. When this computer is switched on it checks the ROMS from right to left. When it detects a suitable ROM it will run the program in that ROM. If the rightmost ROM is BASIC then all will be well, but if it is another language type ROM, e.g. PENDOWN, the computer will simply enter this ROM and PENDOWN will come up on the screen each time you switch on! To avoid this you should ensure that BASIC (the ROM has a number on it ending B01 or B05) is in the rightmost socket. To remove a chip in order to change its position place a small screwdriver under each end alternately and twist it gently. You should lever out each end of the ROM equally or you may bend the pins.
6. The ROM can now be inserted into the computer quite simply as long as care is taken to line the pins up carefully with the socket in the computer. If the rows of pins are splayed out and do not match the socket they can be bent in carefully by resting the ROM on its side on a table and gently bending all the pins on one side of the ROM at once. They should be bent only very slightly. Ensure the pins line up and the ROM is the correct way round (on a BBC B and B + the notch on the end of the ROM should face the back of the computer while on the Master it should face the left side of the machine) and then press the ROM gently but firmly into the chosen socket. Take special care not to bend the pins!

**INSERTING A ROM THE WRONG WAY ROUND
IS LIKELY TO DAMAGE IT PERMANENTLY.**

7. Check that everything is inserted correctly then switch the machine on. It should bleep in the normal way. If it emits a continuous sound then switch off and check that all the ROM's pins are in their correct sockets, then try switching on again. If the fault is still present have the machine checked by a dealer. If everything works normally then type ∗HELP ⟨RETURN⟩ and the computer will display a list of all the ROMs fitted except BASIC. You can then use the computer as normal.

If you are using the BBC Master, ROMs can be fitted without taking the computer apart. The ROM can be inserted in a cartridge which can then be plugged into the slot on the top of the computer. You should switch the machine off before plugging in the cartridge.

The BBC Master also provides the facility to load programs normally found on a chip into a special part of memory called 'sideways RAM'. This means that you can have a copy of the program on a disc and load it into the computer in a similar way to ordinary programs. The command you should use is ∗SRLOAD followed by the name of the program and the address of the sideways RAM. For example, ∗SRLOAD DELTA 8000 4 ⟨RETURN⟩ will load DELTA into RAM area number 4. You could also choose 5, 6 or 7 to specify the sideways RAM area. After loading the program you should press CTRL and tap BREAK so that the computer recognizes the presence of the program in sideways RAM. This process will only work for programs which would normally be found on a ROM. It will not work with programs which are normally loaded from disc.

Using Printers

The most common printers in use in schools are dot-matrix printers. These printers produce their print by causing a series of pins to strike the paper through a ribbon. They are capable of printing text very quickly and using a variety of type styles. This type of printer can also produce a picture of what is on the computer screen — this is called a 'screen dump'. Normally the printer is controlled through the program you are using; you are not expected to be able to cause it to produce fancy output by reading the printer manual.

Most educational programs which use a printer are designed to work with Epson printers. Epson printers are controlled by a specific set of codes which are then used by the programmer to produce the text or graphics they require. In order to get the most out of these programs your printer should be an Epson or Epson-compatible (uses the same codes) printers. Other types of printers are unlikely to work correctly, particularly when dealing with graphics.

When a printer fails to respond as expected the most common problems will be that the printer is not 'on line' or there is no paper present. For the printer to print, it must be plugged into the mains and the appropriate socket under the computer, switched on and have the 'on line' and 'ready' lights illuminated. There will be a small button or pad next to the 'on line' light which switches it 'on line' or 'off line' when pressed. It is also possible for the ribbon to become jammed, although this is unlikely unless the ribbon has been removed and replaced.

If all seems well but the printer is still not working try the printer's self-test routine (how to do this will be explained in the printer's manual).

If the printer has not been used before or has been used with a different type of computer it may be necessary to check that the DIP switches are set correctly for the BBC. The DIP switches are a set of tiny switches which determine the way the printer will behave when used. They set the typeface, page length, line length, character set and various other options. The settings required differ for different computers.

If you are considering changing any of these switches it is essential that you keep a note of how they are set before you make any changes. Only alter these switches if you are sure you need to. Make sure you switch off the power to the printer before changing any switches. One of the most common problems caused by incorrectly set DIP switches is continual over-printing of text on one line. Changing the AUTO LINE FEED switch to on will cure this problem. It is possible to write a simple Basic program to check the normal working of the printer. This should be typed in carefully when you have the normal system prompt (>__) on the screen.

```
10 VDU 2
20 FOR X = 1 TO 20
30 PRINT "This is a printer test"
40 NEXT X
50 VDU 3
```

This should print out twenty lines of 'This is a printer test' one under the other. If they print one on top of another then the AUTO LINE FEED switch is set incorrectly.

There are other printers available for use with the BBC Computer. The most common are daisywheel printers, which perform like electric typewriters and cannot produce graphics, and colour printers, which are particularly good for graphics.

Conclusion

Having some technical knowledge of using the computer can be of use, particularly to sort out those little problems that can arise while the computer is in use. Technical expertise is not, however, a guarantee for good educational use of the computer; it can even get in the way! If after reading this chapter you are still convinced that you could never get to grips with the technical side of things, don't worry, for of course the educational side is far more important.

Appendix A Details of Programs and Special Equipment

Program Details

Program Title	Publisher
AMX Pagemaker	AMX
Caption	MESU
Cars	Cambridgeshire Software House
Colony	MEP
Compose	ITMA
Compose 2	ESP
Composing and Experimenting with Music	Longmans Micro Software
Concept	MESU
Contact	MESU
Datashow	MEP
Delta	Berkshire Education
Developing Tray	Copyright Free
Dinosaur Discovery	4Mation
Dragon World	4Mation
Expedition to Saqqara	Ginn
Extra	MEP
Fairy Tales	RESOURCE
Fleet Street Editor	Mirrorsoft
Flowers of Crystal	4Mation
Folio	Tediman Software
Freewriter	Chris Hopkins
Granny's Garden	4Mation
Grass	Newman College
Image	Cambridge Micro Software
Infant Tray	MEP
Interword	Computer Concepts
Key	ITV Association

List Explorer	MESU
Lost Frog	ESM
Mary Rose	Ginn
Moving In	SEMERC
Ourfacts	MESU
Ourselves	MESU
PenDown	Logotron
Podd	ESM
Police — Language in Evidence	Cambridgeshire Software House
Prompt/Writer	MESU
Quest	AUCBE
Rhythm Maker	ESP
Sorting Game	MESU
Storyline	MEP
Story Starts	Sherston Software
Strategy	MEP
Touch Explorer +	MESU
Typesetter	Sherston Software
Wagons West	4Mation
Window	MESU
Wordplay	BBC Publications
Wordwise Plus	Computer Concepts
World Without Words	4Mation

Publishers' Addresses

Advanced Memory Systems (AMX) Ltd., Green Lane, Appleton, Warrington, WA4 5NG.

AUCBE, Endmion Road, Hatfield, Herts, AL10 8AU.

BBC, 35 Marylebone High Street, London, W1M 4AA.

Berkshire Education Centre for Computers in Education, Fairwater Drive, Woodley, Reading.

Cambridge Micro Software, The Edinburgh Building, Shaftesbury Road, Cambridge.

Cambridgeshire Software House, The Town Hall, St Ives, Huntingdon, Cambridgeshire.

Chris Hopkins, 156 Reading Road, Woodley, Reading, Berkshire.

Computer Concepts, Goddesden Place, Hemel Hempstead, Hertfordshire, HP2 6EX.

ESM, Duke Street, Wisbech, Cambridgeshire, PE13 2AE.

ESP, 75 Beechdale Road, Bilborough, Nottinghamshire.

4Mation Educational Resources, Linden Lea, Rock Park, Barnstaple, Devon, EX32 9AQ

Ginn, Prebendel House, Parson's Fee, Aylesbury, Bucks, HP2 2QZ.

ITMA, The Shell Centre for Mathematical Education, University of Nottingham.

ITV Association Ltd., 6 Paul Street, London EC2.

Logotron Ltd., Dales Brewery, Gwydir Street, Cambridge CB1 2LJ.

Longmans Micro Software, Longman House, Burnt Hill, Harlow, Essex, CM20 2JE.

MEP: programs originally published by the Micro Electronics in Education Project are usually obtainable through Local Education Authorities.

MESU (Micro Electronics Support Unit), Manchester Polytechnic, Hathersage Road, Manchester, M13 0JA.

Mirrorsoft, Headington Hill Hall, Oxford OX3 0BW.

Newman College, Bartley Green, Birmingham, B32 3NT.

RESOURCE, Exeter Road, off Coventry Grove, Doncaster DN2 4PY.

SEMERC (Special Education Micro Electronics Resource Centre), University of Nottingham or University of Manchester.

Sherston Software, Swan Barton, Sherston, Malmesbury, Wiltshire SN16 0LH.

Tediman Software, PO Box 23, Southampton SO9 7BD.

NB Many LEAs can supply programs at a special educational discount. It is therefore advisable to contact the appropriate adviser or computer centre before purchasing programs direct from publishers.

Suppliers of Special Equipment

Concept Keyboards

AB First, Wharfdale Road, Pentwyn, Cardiff, South Glamorgan, CF2 7HB.

Keyboards and Guards

Special Technology Expanded Keyboard for the BBC Micro-computer: Special Technology Ltd., Freepost, Southport, Merseyside, PR8 1BR.

Possum Expanded keyboard for the BBC Microcomputer: Possum Controls Ltd., Middlegreen Trading Estate, Middle-green Road, Langley, Slough, Berks, SL3 6DF.

Keyguard for BBC Microcomputer and Expanded Keyboard: Special Access Systems Ltd., 4 Benson Place, Oxford OX2 6QH.

Electraid Mini Keyboard for BBC computer: JWF Electraid Ltd., Old Exchange, New Street, Aylesbury, Bucks, HP20 2PB.

Guards for Concept Keyboards: Interface Designs, 12 East Meads, Onslow Village, Guildford, Surrey, GU2 5SP.

Speech Synthesizers

Dolphin Mimic: Dolphin Systems, PO Box 83, Worcester WR5 3EQ.

Votrax Type 'n' Talk: Computer Voice Ltd., Cherrytrees, Midwich, Stafford ST18 0EG.

Orovox: Speech System Ltd., Unit 8, Enterprise Row, Range-moor Road, London N15 4NG.

Namal Type & Talk: Cambridge Micro Computer Centre, 153-4 East Road, Cambridge CB1 1DD.

MIDI Interface

Electromusic Research Ltd, 14 Mount Close, Wickford SS11 8HG.

Appendix B Disc Error Messages

David Griffiths

'Bad Address': Occurs when using *LOAD and *SAVE and refers to the numbers required after the commands.

'Bad Attribute': Occurs when using *ACCESS if you use anything other than L or blank after the program name.

'Bad Command': Usually occurs when a * command is mistyped.

'Bad Directory' or **'Bad Dir'**: Usually occurs if you use more than one letter after the *DIR command or you use the forbidden characters ':', '.', '*', '#'.

'Bad Drive': You have used a drive number outside the range 0 to 3 in the commands *BACKUP, *CAT, *COMPACT, *COPY, *DRIVE or as the prefix to a program name where it should be preceded by a ':'.

'Bad Filename' or **'Bad Name'**: You have used an unacceptable name in a command that requires a name. Program names may be preceded by any combination of:

> : Drive No. . Directory .
> e.g. : 1.A.NAME or :1.NAME.

'Bad Option': The number combination in a *OPT command is not permitted.

'Can't Extend': Occurs when a data file or a program is made larger and when re-saved on the disc no longer fits the space allocated to it. Use a different name to avoid the problem.

'Catalogue Full' or **'Cat Full'**: You may only save up to 31 files on a disc. Use another disc.

'Channel': You have used a file handling command incorrectly.

'Disc Changed': Usually occurs when more than one drive is present and the DFS gets confused. Can occur if you change a disc while it is being accessed.

'Disc Fault':

Numbered faults:

&08 — Clock Error
Wrong type of disc.

Disc damaged.

Repeated fault on many discs suggests a computer fault.

Try to ⋆COPY the programs to another disc. Re-format the offending disc. Verify the disc. If still faulty, it should be thrown away.

&0C — Sector Identification error

Wrong type of disc.

Disc damaged.

Repeated fault on many discs suggests a computer fault.

Try to ⋆COPY the programs to another disc. Re-format the offending disc. Verify the disc. If still faulty, it should be thrown away.

&0E — Data Error

Wrong type of disc.

Disc damaged.

Repeated fault on many discs suggests a computer fault.

Try to ⋆COPY the programs to another disc. Re-format the offending disc. Verify the disc. If still faulty it should be thrown away.

&10 — Drive not ready

Disc drive not switched on.

No disc in the drive.

Disc drive chosen (e.g. Drive 1) does not exist.

Hardware faulty.

The remedies for the first three are obvious.

Check the disc cable is connected properly.

Persistent recurrence probably means a faulty disc drive.

&14 — Track 0 not found

Hardware fault.

Persistent recurrence probably means a faulty disc drive.

&16 — Write fault

Hardware fault.

Persistent recurrence probably means a faulty disc drive.

&18 — Sector not found

Very common!

Using the wrong disc format, e.g. forty-track in an eighty-track drive or vice versa.

The disc is unformatted.

The disc is heavily protected to prevent copying.

If not the above then try to ⋆COPY the programs to another disc. Re-format the offending disc. Verify the disc. If still faulty it should be thrown away.

'**Disc Full**': You do not have room on the disc for the file you are trying to save. Use another disc.

'**Disc Read Only**': You have tried to save on a disc which has a 'write protect tab' on it.

'**Drive Fault**': See **Disc Fault**.

'**EOF**': This indicates a programming error in a file handling program.

'**File Exists**' or '**Exists**': Occurs when you try to rename a file using a name that already exists on the disc. Choose a new name or delete the existing file.

'**File Locked**' or '**Locked**': You have tried to save onto or delete a file locked by ⋆ACCESS. Unlock the file using ⋆ACCESS.

'**File not Found**' or '**Not Found**': The DFS cannot find the file you have asked for on the disc. Most probably you have either misspelt the name or have the wrong disc in the drive.

'**File Open**' or '**Open**': Usually caused by a programming error in a file handling program. Typing CLOSE#0 will close all files.

'**File Read Only**' or '**Read Only**': Usually caused by a programming error in a file handling program.

'**Locked**': See '**File Locked**'

'**Not Enabled**' (**DFS 0.90 only**): You have typed ⋆BACKUP or ⋆DESTROY without first typing ⋆ENABLE.

'**Open**': See '**File Open**'.

'**Read Only**': See '**File Read Only**'.

'**Syntax**': You have got a DFS command wrong. Check the syntax in a User Guide.

'**Too Many Open Files**' or '**Too Many Open**': Usually caused by a programming error in a file handling program.

Hardware Problems

If you suspect your disc drive or computer may be faulty try them out with a friend's system that you know is working before incurring any repair bills.

Notes on Contributors

David Congdon took a degree in Music Education before taking up his first post in a 9–13 middle school. At present he is head of the lower junior team in a large new primary school, and has particular responsibility for Music and CDT. He has always seen an important place for computers in the primary school and has run a number of courses on the subject. In his spare time he enjoys playing keyboards in a dinner dance band.

David Cowell is currently appointed to the Devon Education Authority with a responsibility to explore a cross-curricular approach for Educational Technology. The early part of his life was spent as a joiner and woodcarver, restoring churches and other buildings and he therefore began teaching rather later after taking a fine art course at St Luke's College. He taught in various primary schools before being presented with a ZX81 in 1981. This prompted an interest in computers in education which has been sustained and which has led to his present post.

Rob Crompton is a lecturer in education at the University of Reading. He has taught in a variety of primary schools in Manchester, Middlesborough, Cambridgeshire and Berkshire, and was head of two contrasting schools: a small village primary and a large new open-plan school. He has wide-ranging interests and has written scripts for children's television and for a schools television geography series. He has also composed two 'rock operas' for children and maintains an interest in popular music through both recording and performing.

Howard Gillings was trained as a drama teacher at Bulmershe College more years ago then he cares to remember and is currently the headteacher of Crown Wood Primary School in Bracknell. He has had an involvement in computing in primary schools since the early 1970s, and welcomes the accessibility of powerful machines to all teachers. He is actively involved in INSET work for Information Technology and spends a great deal of his time endeavouring to 'demystify' computers and all that they involve. He is married with two children and indulges what little spare time that he has in railway modelling.

David Griffiths has taught in a wide variety of schools during the past twenty years and is currently headteacher at Stokenham Primary School in South Devon. He spent a number of years as a teaching head in Berkshire where he was engaged in various County initiatives in Computing and CDT. As a founder member of the Primary Computer Support Team he was involved in designing, delivering and evaluating in-service work for teachers for over five years. During this time he was seconded on two occasions, firstly to lecture on IT in primary schools at Bulmershe College of Higher Education, and more recently to the Education Office in Berkshire to work with the administrative officers and the advisory service.

Chris Hopkins has been involved with computers and special education for the last five years. She is currently a support teacher for Computers and Special Needs and has used her programming expertise in the production of new programs and the adaptation of existing ones to cater for children who have difficulties in using standard software. She has also adapted some of the more popular BBC programs to run on the new generation computers. She was at one time head of Biology at a North London School teaching Biology and Integrated Science and has also spent three years in The Netherlands where she worked in adult education, teaching English as a foreign language.

Monica Hughes is a lecturer in Early Childhood Education at the University of Reading where she is involved with the BEd and PGCE programmes of initial training. She has a particular commitment to the integrated curriculum while maintaining an interest in Religious Education in the primary school. Her previous experience includes being a first school headteacher, primary advisory teacher and Schools Council project officer. She has written on a variety of subjects for educational journals and was a major contributor to *Match and Mismatch: Raising Questions/Finding Answers*, Oliver and Boyd, 1977.

Anthony Hunt's background is firmly rooted in primary education. After teaching in East Sussex, Kent and Bromley he became head of a primary school in Hampshire in 1981. Around that time he attended his first computer course for primary teachers and became interested in the use of computers to enhance and extend the curriculum. This interest developed when he became a microtrainer on the DTI induction scheme and was involved in many educational initiatives. In 1987 he was appointed as Primary IT Development Coordinator for Hampshire's 600 primary establishments and is currently working on the development of the ESG programme. He is particularly keen to explore the skills that children develop through using IT in the primary curriculum.

Philip Mann has worked in ILEA specializing in maths and science in the primary curriculum. He has been teaching in Berkshire for ten years and for the last five years has been the headteacher of a primary school in Thatcham. Apart from an interest in Art and CDT, he is a member of the county's Computer Support Team and has organized courses in diverse curriculum areas, including language. Although his two young children take up much of his spare time, he does manage to spend some time pursuing his interest in photography.

Denby Richards is head of a 5–12 combined school in Berkshire. Prior to this he worked variously as a class teacher, deputy head and probationary teacher tutor. Although a Luddite at heart and suspicious of technology he became converted after seeing a 'Pet' in action in 1980. He purchased a machine for his school but until the formation of MEP he was singularly unimpressed with the general standard of the available software. He joined the Berkshire Computer Support Team at its inception and is firmly wedded to its basic philosophy that computers are merely tools to enhance the best of established primary practice.

Tim Royle studied at Stourbridge College of Art and Design and at the Royal College of Art. He has a wide range of teaching experience and is currently General Adviser with responsibility for art and design in Berkshire. He has been actively involved in promoting the use of computers in the art and design curriculum and has generated considerable interest amongst students, teachers and educationalists. He has worked with both the BBC and ITV, and was recently involved in the BBC Schools programme 'Micro Mindstretchers', which featured primary school children using computers in art and design.

Ann Snowdon has worked as a class teacher in nursery, infant, and primary schools and is currently deputy head of a newly opened primary school in Thatcham. She was a member of the Berkshire Theatre in Education team for five years, working on a variety of programmes written for primary school children. This resulted in a six-part schools radio programme and led to the establishment of a full-time group of teachers known as Learning Through Action. After some time as a member of the local computer support group she was seconded to work in an advisory capacity supporting the use of computers across the primary curriculum. She continues to run INSET courses and is also involved in courses in school management team teaching, and the teaching of reading.

Sue Underhay is currently seconded as an Advisory Teacher for Information Technology with Berkshire Education Authority, and is also a member of the county's Primary Computer Support team. She has taught in Berkshire for twelve years, during which time she has worked in both large urban and small country schools. Her teaching experience has been across the Primary age range, including many years with mixed age groups. At different times she has held posts of responsibility for a variety of curriculum areas including Language, Science and latterly, Computers across the Curriculum.

DEPARTMENT OF EDUCATION